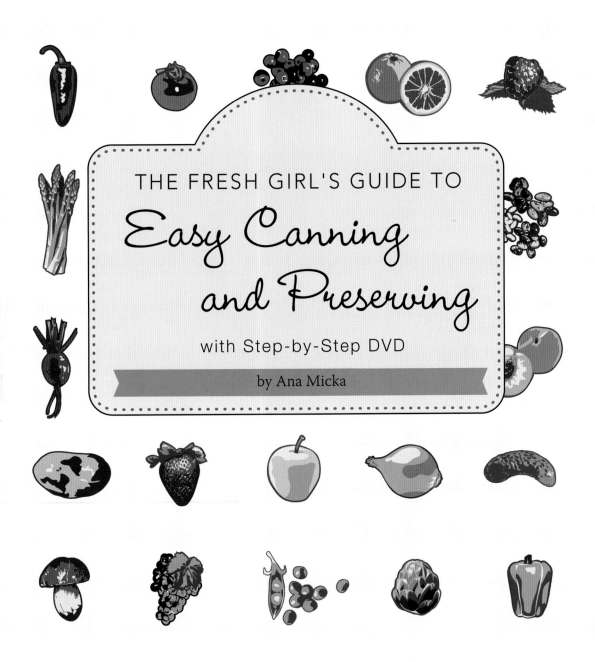

THE FRESH GIRL'S GUIDE TO

Easy Canning

and Preserving

with Step-by-Step DVD

by Ana Micka

Voyageur Press

First published in 2010 by Voyageur Press, an imprint of MBI Publishing Company,
400 First Avenue North, Suite 300, Minneapolis, MN 55401 USA

Voyageur Press titles are also available at discounts in bulk quantity for industrial or
sales-promotional use. For details write to Special Sales Manager at MBI Publishing
Company, 400 First Avenue North, Suite 300, Minneapolis, MN 55401 USA.

To find out more about our books, visit us online at www.voyageurpress.com.

ISBN-13: 978-0-7603-3846-9

Editor: Kari Cornell
Design Manager: Katie Sonmor
Designed by: Aleksandra Till, Entropy Design Lab
DVD Credits: Gabe Cheifetz, 612 Authentic Media; edits by Anne Breckenridge, Greatapes, Inc.
Host: Leigha Horton

Printed in China

  Library of Congress Cataloging-in-Publication Data

Micka, Ana, 1969-
  The fresh girl's guide to easy canning and preserving / Ana Micka.
      p. cm.
  ISBN 978-0-7603-3846-9 (flexibound)
  1. Canning and preserving. 2. Food--Preservation. I. Title.
  TX603.M42 2010
  641.4'2--dc22
  2009043033

Do you want to eat locally grown food, support family farmers, and save money on food? Here's how: learn to can!

I taught myself to can ten years ago in order to use locally grown food and reduce additives in my family's diet. I started with the basics: jam and stewed tomatoes. I've now expanded my repertoire to include recipes and flavors from around the globe.

I also quickly learned how to use a pressure canner, my favorite kitchen tool. I recouped the cost in one canning season. With the pressure canner, I can make the most of fresh, in-season vegetables from the garden and market. Best of all, the pressure canner allows me to can meals in a jar, including soups, chili, and even pulled pork. During the busy school year, it's a great relief and joy to open the cupboard and have dinner on hand.

The Fresh Girl's Guide to Easy Canning and Preserving gives you all the information you need to start canning today. I'll show you the basic steps to home canning and provide four simple rules for safely canning foods. The enclosed DVD allows you to see the process and learn by watching—giving you even more confidence as you head into the kitchen.

In my own kitchen I focus on healthy foods, so I asked expert canner Paula Pentel to share her Minnesota State Fair award-winning applesauce recipe and her personal recipe for low-sugar strawberry jam. Yum!

So peruse the recipes in this book, pop in *The Fresh Girl's Guide to Easy Canning and Preserving* DVD, and enjoy the best of what the harvest has to offer.

—Ana

Home Canning's 15 Minutes of Fame

Home canning was a badge of patriotism during World War II. Major public relations campaigns encouraged Americans to plant Victory Gardens and can their own food to keep fruits and vegetables affordable during the war. According to Rose Hayden-Smith, a leading victory garden historian and director of the University of California Cooperative Extension in Ventura County, more than twenty million gardens were planted in backyards and vacant lots during World War II. These gardens produced up to forty percent of all the vegetable produce consumed nationally!

Canning is regaining popularity today for many reasons.

2,000 Miles Closer to Home

Home canning is a great way to reduce your carbon footprint. Produce in the United States typically travels 1,300 to 2,000 miles (about 2,000 to 3,200 km) from farm to table. Eighty percent of the energy used in the food sector goes toward processing, transportation, and storage.

Dollars spent to buy produce directly from farmers create a stronger local economy. Plus fresh, local food just tastes better.

Good Food at Affordable Prices

Home canning is a sure way to avoid corn syrup, industrial oils, additives, and high levels of sodium. My daughter is on a gluten-free diet and canning gives me confidence in the foods I prepare for her.

Of course, canning is also a sure way to eat locally grown food year-round without blowing your budget. Produce is abundant and very affordable when it's in season. A quart of filling squash soup can cost you only seventy-five cents to prepare, and spaghetti sauce can be as low as a dollar per jar. I'll give you suggestions for finding great produce and some tips on how to grow your own.

If you have a sunny space in your yard or are lucky enough to have access to a community garden, prepare the soil and grow your own canning garden using these tips and guides.

Tomatoes

Tomatoes are by far the most popular garden plant. The best varieties for canning are the Roma (plum) tomatoes. These smaller, oval tomatoes have more meat, fewer seeds, and pack a lot of rich tomato flavor into your jars. Romas are also "determinate" tomatoes, meaning they tend to ripen at or near the same time. This can be a benefit when you're harvesting for the purpose of canning. Other tomatoes such as Celebrity, Brandywine, and similar hybrid and heirloom varieties also work well.

Tomato planting guidelines:
You'll need about 3 pounds (1.4 kg) of tomatoes for each quart (about a liter) of canned tomatoes. For a canner batch of 7 quarts (6.6 l), plan on planting the following quantities of tomato plants:

* Roma tomato plants: Plant 3–4 plants for a 7-quart (6.6 l) canning recipe. Each plant yields 6–8 pounds (2.7–3.6 kg) of fruit on average.
* Celebrity/Brandywine tomato plants: Plant 2–3 plants for 7 quarts (6.6 l). Each plant yields 8–12 pounds (3.6–5.4 kg) of fruit on average.

Plant your tomatoes 18–36 inches (45.8–91.4 cm) apart in soil prepared with compost. Tomatoes require a lot of nutrients, so I recommend adding 5–6 pounds (2.3–2.7 kg) of compost for every square foot (30.5 square centimeters) of garden space. Tomatoes also need sun, so plant them where they will receive 7 hours of sunlight each day. Water, mulch, and stake your plants, and in 2 or 3 months you'll be harvesting!

The smaller tomato varieties can be planted in containers. This can be a good option for Roma tomato plants if you have limited growing room. Containers do not work well with the larger, heritage plant varieties. To learn more about planting in containers, see page 12.

Vegetables

Beans, beets, carrots, corn, cucumbers, potatoes, and squash round out your canning garden. Plant plenty—if you have room!

Get creative with your space. Increase your harvest by growing beans and squash vertically and make use of containers. See tips for growing container gardens on page 12.

Plan for succession planting. In most climates, you will be able to plant several crops of beans and possibly even beets and carrots. A fall crop of beans, for example, can be planted in garden spaces emptied by mid-season harvesting.

If you need space, find and join a community garden in your area.

The website www.communitygarden.org lists many gardens across the country. Also call your city, township, or local neighborhood association, as many gardens are not listed.

Friends and neighbors who have larger yards may also be open to a sharing arrangement.

Fruits

If you have enough space and plan to stay for a while, planting fruit trees, bushes, and plants is very rewarding. They are often beautiful additions to your yard and can provide significant cost savings.

Look into edible landscaping and permaculture gardening for ways to introduce fruits throughout your yard. Dwarf apple bushes, blueberry bushes, and strawberries can easily be incorporated into eye-pleasing landscapes, even in front yards!

Only have space for a small garden?

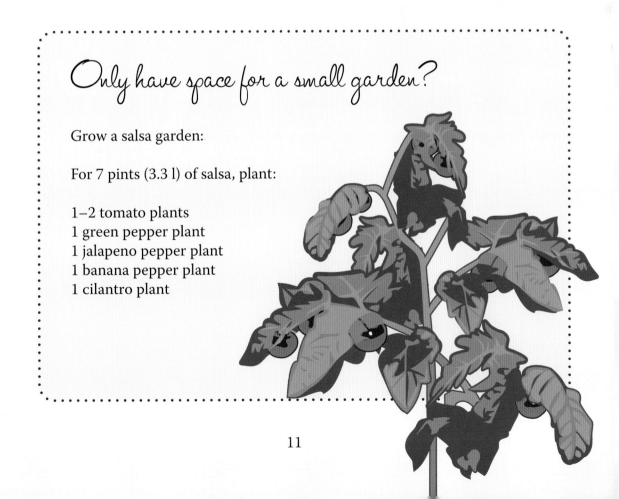

Grow a salsa garden:

For 7 pints (3.3 l) of salsa, plant:

1–2 tomato plants
1 green pepper plant
1 jalapeno pepper plant
1 banana pepper plant
1 cilantro plant

Growing a Canning Garden

Planting in Containers

Container gardening can be a great way to expand your garden harvest. You can grow smaller varieties of tomatoes and common canning vegetables like cucumbers, beans, and peppers. Here are a few tips for a successful growing season:

* Choose a container large enough for your plants. Five- to six-gallon (19–23 l) pots work fine for most vegetables. Drainage is critical. Make sure your pots have drain holes and add an inch (2.5 cm) of gravel to the bottom of the pot to help drain the soil.

* Use soil specifically made for containers. Potting soil is a lightweight, sterile mix. This kind of soil helps retain moisture and remains pliable over time. Do not use regular garden soil in your containers—it will eventually become hard and compacted and strangle your plant's roots.

* Water frequently. Plants grown in containers dry out very quickly. Vegetables in general (tomatoes in particular) need a regular, often daily, source of water.

* Feed your plants. Nutrients in containers are washed away when you water your plants. Fertilize frequently; weekly fertilization is recommended. You can use a variety of fertilizers—your local garden center should have both organic and regular fertilizer options.

My family ends up devouring most of the fresh vegetables we grow in our community garden plot. I buy most of my produce for canning directly from farmers. You can find great deals when crops are at the peak of their season, especially if you purchase in bulk—a great strategy for canning!

Farmers' Markets

Most communities now have farmers' markets. According the USDA, Agricultural Marketing Service, there are 5,246 recognized farmers' markets in the United States that provide a wide variety of seasonal, locally grown fruits and vegetables. You can save a bundle by buying in bulk, so make sure to ask the farmers if they have bulk pricing.

To locate farmers' markets in your area, visit www.LocalHarvest.org, a great website that lists many local farms, shops, and other resources. The USDA also has a list of farmers' markets: www.apps.ams.usda.gov/FarmersMarkets.

Note: Many farmer's markets now accept WIC and food stamps. This can be a great way to stretch these resources and keep fruits and veggies on the table year-round.

Pick-Your-Own Farms

Visiting pick-your-own farms is the best way to get the freshest fruit in bulk—and it's fun! Pick-your-own farms are located throughout the United States and outside most metropolitan areas. Berries and apples are the most popular crops.

The website www.pickyourown.org has a list of farms by state. If you search the Internet using the keyword "pick your own" with the name of your state, you will also find listings.

Buying Produce

For the most fun, plan an outing with family and friends to an apple orchard or berry patch, then invite them all over for a canning party afterwards to make apple sauce or jam.

CSAs (Community Supported Agriculture)

CSAs have become a popular way for individuals to purchase produce directly from farmers. Most CSA farms offer shares at the beginning of each season. You pay a fixed, seasonal price and in return receive a portion of the harvest—usually a beautiful box of vegetables—each week during the growing season. Most CSAs offer vegetables, but some offer fruits, dairy, and meat. Often, a CSA share will provide plenty of produce for small-batch canning. Many CSAs are now also offering *canning shares*, which are larger deliveries of in-season produce specifically for canning. Contact local CSAs to see if they have canning shares available in your area.

To find a CSA and learn more about the CSA model, visit:
The CSA Center: www.csacenter.org
Local Harvest: www.localharvest.org

Canning is much easier and safer if you make use of the equipment readily available in your local hardware, farm, or home supply store (like Fleet Farm, for example), or online. Jars, lids, and canning-specific ingredients like pectin are available at most grocery stores.

Hot Water Bath Canner

A large pot with a canning rack and a lid. Canning pots are usually 21 or 33 quarts (about 20 or 31 liters). You can use regular pots with lids as long as they are large enough to allow for at least 2 inches (5 cm) of water over the jars.

Pressure Canner

A large aluminum pot with a twist-on, locking lid, inner sealing rim, a rack, and a pressure gauge. The most popular pressure canner sizes are 16 or 22 quarts (about 15 or 21 liters). The smaller pressure cookers, usually 4-, 6-, or 8-quart (3.8, 5.7, or 7.6 liter) sizes, are great for daily cooking but are not approved for home canning.

Canning Rack

Most canners come with a canning rack. The rack for hot water bath canners has slots for the jars and handles to lift the rack in and out of the canner. Pressure canners come with flat, plate-style racks that sit at the bottom of the canner. A rack protects the jars from direct heat on the bottom of the pan and prevents them from bouncing around during processing. Make sure to use a canning rack every time you can!

Canning Equipment

Jars
Use only jars made for canning, such as those made by Mason or Ball. Jar sizes range from 4 ounces (118 ml) to a quart (about a liter). Jars come in both wide- and regular-mouth sizes.

Lids
Use only the two-part lid made for canning jars. You must use new rubber-sealed lid tops every time you can (called dome or mason lids). You can reuse the outer screw rings.

Funnel
With an opening sized for canning jars.

Jar Lifter
Used for removing hot jars from boiling water.

Clean Towels and Potholders
Nothing fancy needed here, just make sure the towels are clean.

Sauce or Stock Pans
Stainless-steel or enamel-surfaced pans work best when preparing recipes for canning. Aluminum and copper pans are considered "reactive" and will impart a metallic taste to acidic foods.

Candy Thermometer
Useful for making jams.

Thin Rubber Spatula or Chopsticks
Used to remove air bubbles before processing.

This section will demystify the canning process, and put to rest notions that canning is hard, complicated, or dangerous. I encourage you to watch the "Safety First" segment on the DVD, where Julie Ristau, a canning safety expert, makes it easy to can with confidence. Julie grew up canning with her grandmother on the family farm and has a degree in Home Economics from Iowa State University. Here's what she has to say:

"There are really just four simple steps to safe canning—and since they all begin with the letter *S* they are a snap to remember."

The four simple steps to safe canning:

Sterilize

Select

Seal

Store

Safety First

1. Sterilize

Take a few minutes to complete these important steps at the beginning of any canning session.

Basic steps:

1. Boil water. Submerge all jars, lids, and any kitchen tools you will be using for 2 minutes in boiling water.

2. Gather clean towels for the countertops and for wiping down the jars.

3. Clean kitchen surfaces with hot water and a touch of vinegar.

4. Make sure your hands are squeaky clean.

2. Select

Not all foods are canned the same way. Some use a hot water bath canner and others require a pressure canner. It's important to know which canning method you will be using and to have the proper equipment. I'll show you how to use both.

Foods with a low pH (meaning they are more acidic) require the basic, hot water bath method where the water reaches 212 degrees Fahrenheit, or boiling temperature. Fruits, tomatoes with added acid, and pickles can be canned this way.

Higher pH foods (foods that are less acidic) require a pressure canner, which reaches 240 degrees Fahrenheit. Higher pH foods require the increased temperature to kill off all bacteria, so it's important to follow the selection guidelines carefully. Vegetables, meats, and any stocks or soups must be processed using a pressure canner.

What's pH?

All cooking is chemistry—and in canning, it's the pH value of your food that matters most.

The simplest way to remember pH is that **fruits, pickled foods** and **tomatoes with added vinegar or lemon juice** (high-acid foods) use a **hot water bath canning method.** Everything else needs a **pressure canner,** which reaches 240 degrees Fahrenheit to kill off all bacteria.

Why is this? It's because the dreaded botulism-causing bacteria don't survive in foods with a pH of 4.6 or less, so it's safe to process them in boiling water with a temperature of 212 degrees Fahrenheit. Other foods require higher temperatures to be safely processed.

Determine Canning Method

High-acid foods like fruits, pickled foods, and tomatoes

Use a Hot Water Bath

Low-acid foods such as vegetables, meats, and soups

Use a Pressure Canner
10 lbs pressure kills botulism
*Remember to heat all low-acid foods before eating.

Chart 1: pH Value of Various Foods

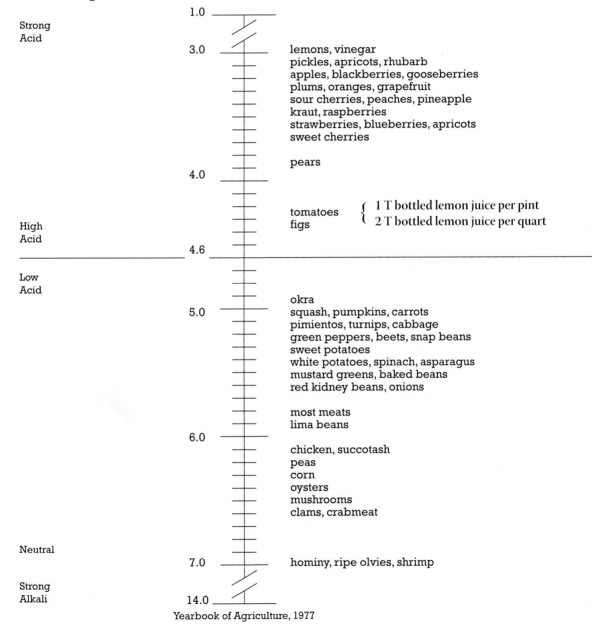

Strong
Acid

1.0

3.0 — lemons, vinegar
pickles, apricots, rhubarb
apples, blackberries, gooseberries
plums, oranges, grapefruit
sour cherries, peaches, pineapple
kraut, raspberries
strawberries, blueberries, apricots
sweet cherries

pears

4.0

tomatoes   { 1 T bottled lemon juice per pint
figs   { 2 T bottled lemon juice per quart

High
Acid

4.6

Low
Acid

okra
5.0 — squash, pumpkins, carrots
pimientos, turnips, cabbage
green peppers, beets, snap beans
sweet potatoes
white potatoes, spinach, asparagus
mustard greens, baked beans
red kidney beans, onions

most meats
lima beans

6.0

chicken, succotash
peas
corn
oysters
mushrooms
clams, crabmeat

Neutral
7.0 — hominy, ripe olvies, shrimp

Strong
Alkali
14.0

Yearbook of Agriculture, 1977

Chart 2: Temperatures for Food Preservation

Canning temperature for low acid vegetables, meat and poultry in a pressure canner —— 240° F

Water boils: Canning temperature for high acid fruits, tomatoes, pickles and jellied products in a boiling water bath canner —— 212° F

Average simmer —— 190° F

165° F

Temperature for drying foods in an oven or dehydrator —— 140° F

Cooking temperatures destroy most bacteria, yeasts and molds. Time required to kill these decrease as temperatures increase.

Warming temperatures prevent growth but may allow survival of some microorganisms.

DANGER ZONE: Temperatures in this zone allow rapid growth of bacteria, yeasts and molds, and production of toxins by some bacteria and molds.

80° F

Average room temperatures

60° F

Best storage temperatures for canned and dried food

50° F

40° F

Water freezes —— 32° F

Cold temperatures permit slow growth of some bacteria, yeasts and molds.

Best storage temperatures for frozen foods

0° F

-10° F

Freezing temperatures stop growth of microorganisms, but may allow some to survive.

3. Seal

Sealing occurs when a jar covered with a dome lid is processed in either a hot water bath or a pressure canner. Ensuring you have a good, tight seal is critical to preserving your food.

Each lid has two parts—an outer ring and an inner panel with a rubber seal. Make sure both parts are sterilized and intact. The outer rings may be reused, but be sure to use new dome lids every time you can.

A few tips to ensure a good seal:

Make sure to leave the recommended amount of headspace in your jar. Headspace is the amount of room left between the top of the food and lid. Too much room, and your food will spoil on top; too little room and a vacuum seal cannot be created. Strong acid foods need ¼" headspace, low acid foods need ½" headspace.

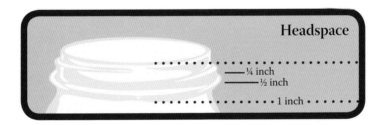

Headspace

¼ inch
½ inch

1 inch

Once jars have processed and cooled, turn upside down to check for leaks. Make sure each one is sealed by pressing slightly on the center of the dome lid. If the lid makes a hollow popping sound and moves up and down, it isn't sealed. When this happens, refrigerate the jar and eat the contents within two weeks.

4. Store

Just two simple steps here:

First—Make sure to label your jars with the canning date and contents. Home-canned food will last up to twelve months.

Second—Store your canned jars in a cool, dark spot. Never store cans near a heat source, such as hot pipes, furnace vents or radiators, or a sunny window. This will harm the quality of your food.

I invert my canning jars for storage. This keeps the top layer of the food from drying out. Before storing jars, remove screw-top rings.

What Can I Can?

A quick summary of what we've learned so far:

In a hot water bath you can can:
  All fruits
  Tomatoes with extra acid (lemon juice or vinegar) added
  Pickles

In a pressure cooker you can can:
  Vegetables (beets, carrots, potatoes, squash cubes)
  Beans
  Meats
  Stocks and brothy soups

Do NOT can:
  Grains and starches (including rice and pasta, even if they're in soups)
  Oils
  Dairy products
  Pureed winter squash or pumpkin (see recipe on page 71 for a solution)
  Thickeners, such as cornstarch or flour

When you can, ALWAYS:
  * Use fresh ingredients. Any blemishes on produce should be cut out.
  * Follow all directions and recipes to the letter.
  * Know your altitude and adjust processing instructions accordingly.
  * Sterilize your jars, lids, and equipment before you begin.
  * Keep a journal—it's great to have as a guide for next time.
  * Have fun!

Let's Can!... Using the Hot Water Bath Method

Before you begin, gather the necessary equipment. To can using the hot water bath method, you will need a canner, canning rack, jars, lids, funnel, jar lifter, sauce or stock pans, and possibly a candy thermometer. See Canning Equipment on page 15–16 for details.

We will explore fruit recipes in this chapter, including:

Whole Fruits & Sauces
Fruit Jams & Preserves
Tomatoes
Pickles

Hot Water Bath Method

Follow these basic steps to make home canning simple and safe:

1. Follow the sterilization instructions on page 18.

2. Fill your hot water bath canner two-thirds full with water and bring to a boil. You want enough water so that when you submerge the jars, the water level remains 2 inches (5 cm) above the lids. Adding vinegar (2 tablespoons [30 ml] or a good splash) helps if you have hard water. Minerals in hard water tend to form a cloudy surface on your jars. Vinegar helps keep the minerals in the water and off your jars.

3. Prepare your canning recipe, using only recipes meant for home canning. Fill your sterilized jars with the food, leaving the recommended amount of headspace. Use a non-reactive kitchen utensil, such as narrow rubber spatula or a bamboo skewer, to remove air bubbles. Air bubbles can cause uneven heating during processing and may impair the jar's ability to seal. Using a clean towel or paper towel, wipe the rims of the jars. This removes any spilled liquid or food, which can also prevent the jar from sealing. Place a dome lid on top of the jar and secure with a jar ring, screwing on so it's secure but not tight.

4. Submerge jars into canner with boiling water. Water should be 2 inches (5 cm) above the tops of the jars. ALWAYS place jars on a rack. If you don't have the rack made specifically for your canner, use a steamer basket or some other method to elevate the jars off the bottom of the canner. Jars that come into contact with direct heat through the bottom of the canning pot can crack and break.

5. Place lid on canning pot. Once the water returns to a boil, begin timing. Process for the number of minutes specified by the recipe, adjusting for altitude if necessary.

6. Once the processing time has elapsed, use the jar lifter to remove the jars from the boiling water. Place them on a towel on your countertop and let them rest until cooled. After 24 hours, test the seals by pressing slightly on the center of the dome lid. If the lid makes a hollow popping sound and moves up and down, it isn't sealed. When this happens, refrigerate the jar and eat the contents within 2 weeks. Make sure to label canned foods with the recipe name and date the item was canned. Store in a cool, dry place. Eat within a year.

About Altitude

Altitude matters for cooking in general and home canning in particular. Altitude affects the cooking temperature, so take a moment to look up your altitude (also called elevation) and follow the canning instructions accordingly. EarthTools (www.earthtools.org) has an altitude reference section that's searchable by city.

If you live in an area with an altitude above 1,000 feet (305 m), increase processing time by 2 minutes for every 1,000 (305 m) additional feet above sea level when using the hot water bath method.

For pressure canning, you will need to increase the pressure settings for areas in higher altitudes. See page 64 for guidelines.

Hot Water Bath Method

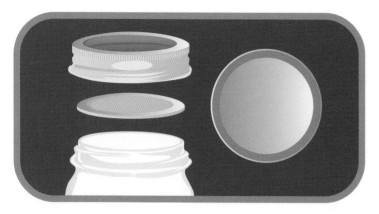

1 Sterilize equipment and cooking area (see page 18 for sterilization instructions).

2 Fill canner ⅔ full with water. Add 2 tablespoons (30 ml) white vinegar. Bring to boil.

3 Prepare recipe. Fill jars, leaving proper headspace. Remove air bubbles. Wipe rims, seal with lids.

4 Submerge jars and canning rack into canning pot. Make sure water level is 2 inches (5 cm) above jar lids.

5 Once water returns to a boil, process jars for specified time (to adjust for altitude, see page 29).

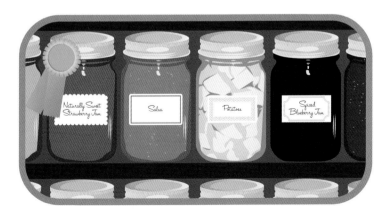

6 Remove jars, let cool on a countertop. Test seals. Label and store. Refrigerate any jars that haven't sealed properly and eat within 2 weeks.

Whole and Sliced Fruits and Sauces

Fruits need to be canned in liquid. Depending on your taste preferences and the tartness of the fruit, select one of the fruit syrup options from page 33. Sugar helps fruit hold its shape and color, but sugar-free recipes can also work. Each recipe asks you to refer to and select one of these options. You'll need enough liquid to completely cover the fruit once it's jarred.

This section includes recipes for:

Citrus Fruits
Fruit with Pits or a Core
Sauces

Applesauce

Grapefruit, Oranges, Tangerines

10–12 pounds (4.5–5.4 kg) of
fruit makes about 5 quarts (4.7 l)

1. Prepare for canning
   (follow steps 1 and 2 from
   the Hot Water Bath
   Method, page 28).
2. Remove skin, segment
   fruit, and remove white
   membrane and seeds.
3. Select and prepare a
   fruit syrup option (see
   right). Bring to a boil.
4. Pack fruit into sterilized jars
   and cover with boiling syrup,
   leaving a ½-inch (1.3 cm)
   headspace. Use a nonmetallic
   spatula or skewer to
   remove air bubbles. Secure
   lid and screw ring.
5. Place jars in canner on
   canning rack. Make sure
   water level is 2 inches (5 cm)
   above the tops of the jars.
   Return the water to a boil.
6. Process jars at a boil for
   10 minutes. If you live
   in a high-altitude area,
   increase the processing
   time by 2 minutes for
   every 1,000 feet (304.8 m)
   above sea level you are.

Fruit syrup options
(choose one)

Makes enough for 8 pints
or 4 quarts (3.8 l) of
canned fruit pieces

Boiling water (enough to cover
your fruit and fill the jar)
2 cups (383 g) sugar plus
7 cups (1.8 l) water (this
will make a very light syrup,
so add more sugar if you
prefer a sweeter, heavier
syrup or your fruit is tart)

3 C juice (750 ml) (apple,
grape, or juice of the
fruit you're canning)
+ 4 T (60 ml) lemon juice
+ 5 C (1.3 l) water

2 C juice (500 ml) (apple,
grape, or juice of the
fruit you're canning)
+ 1 C (250 ml) honey
+ 4 ½ C (1.1 l) water

33

Fruit with Pits or a Core

Apples, Apricots, Cherries*, Nectarines, Pears, Peaches, Pineapples, Plums

10–12 pounds (4.5–5.4 kg) of fruit makes about 4 quarts (3.8 l)

1. Prepare for canning (follow steps 1 and 2 from the Hot Water Bath Canning Method, page 28).
2. Peel apples, pears, and pineapples. Remove cores. Remove skins of peaches by submerging in boiling water for 20 seconds. Do not peel nectarines, apricots, plums, or cherries. Halve or slice fruit and remove any seeds or pits (plums are best left whole, but prick both ends to prevent bursting). Prevent discoloration by soaking light-colored fruit (apples, apricots, nectarines, pears, and peaches) in an ascorbic acid solution for 2 minutes, leaving in liquid until ready to can (see tip on page 35).
3. Select a fruit syrup option from page 33. Prepare syrup by combining ingredients in a stainless-steel or enamel pan. Bring to a boil, then reduce heat to bring liquid to a simmer.
4. Add fruit and cook at a simmer for 5 minutes.
5. Pack into hot jars, leaving a ½-inch (1.3 cm) headspace. Add more boiling water or syrup if necessary to fill jar and cover fruit. Use a nonmetallic spatula or skewer to remove air bubbles. Secure lid and screw ring.
6. Place jars in canner on canning rack. Make sure water level is 2 inches (5 cm) above the tops of the jars. Return the water to a boil.
7. Process jars at a boil, quart-sized (946 ml) jars for 25 minutes (*20 minutes for cherries), pint-sized (473 ml) jars for 20 minutes (*15 minutes for cherries). If you live in a high-altitude area, increase the processing time by 2 minutes for every 1,000 feet (305 m) above sea level you are.

Variation: Adding liquor to your fruit is a nice way to make your preserves extra special during the holidays. After cooking fruit in sugar syrup, pack fruit into jar, add a tablespoon (15 ml) of rum or brandy OR 1 ½ teaspoons (7.5 ml) of port or Grand Marnier, then fill with fruit sugar syrup, leaving a ½-inch (1.3 cm) headspace. Process as usual.

Prevent Discoloration

Soak light-colored produce like apples, peaches, pears, nectarines, and apricots in an ascorbic acid solution to keep from browning. Powdered ascorbic acid or crushed Vitamin C tablets are the best and easiest way to prevent fruit from darkening. This is a simple, but important step. Here's how:

1. Crush three 500 mg Vitamin C tablets into 2 quarts (1.9 l) of cold water and add fruit.
2. Soak for at least 2 minutes. Keep fruit in solution until you're ready to use it.

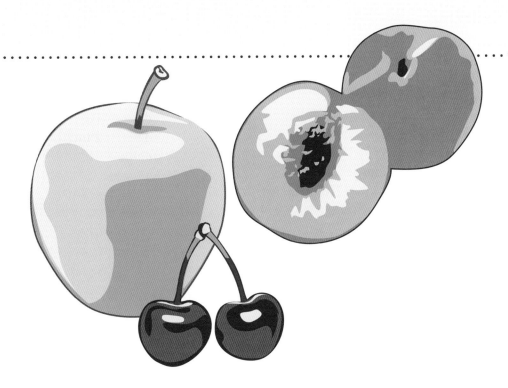

State Fair Applesauce by Paula Pentel and Callie Wilson

Makes 5 pints (2.4 l)

Paula Pentel and Callie Wilson are an award-winning canning team with the ribbons to prove it. Here's their applesauce recipe, which took second place at the Minnesota State Fair in 2006! The recipe is sugar free, but no one will ever know. You can watch Paula and Callie make this recipe on the *Fresh Girl's Guide to Easy Canning and Preserving* DVD.

24 apples (mix 2–3 different varieties if possible)
Water
1 T (15 ml) ground cinnamon (or to taste)
5 t (25 ml) lemon juice

1. Follow steps 1 and 2 from the Hot Water Bath Method (see page 28).
2. Wash, core, and cut apples. *Note*: In the DVD Paula uses a handy food strainer. If you do not have a food strainer, simply peel the apples with a paring knife.
3. Place the apples in a heavy-bottomed, non-reactive pot (stainless-steel or enamel). Add a small amount of water, about an inch (2.5 cm). Cook apples until soft, 15–20 minutes.
4. Strain or mash cooked apples (if not using a food mill, mash by hand or use a blender or food processor to create desired consistency).
5. Add cinnamon if desired.
6. Use a measuring cup or ladle and a funnel to fill jars with applesauce. Leave a ½-inch (1.3 cm) headspace at the top of the jar. Use a nonmetallic spatula or skewer to remove air bubbles. Secure lid and screw ring.
7. Place jars into the canning rack and lower into boiling water in the canner. Cover, return to a boil, and process for 20 minutes, adjusting for altitude if necessary (see page 29).
    Note: Do not start your timer until the water returns to a boil.

Cranberry Sauce

Makes 4 pints (1.9 l)

This sauce is a great treat for the holidays!

2 C (500 ml) orange juice
2 C (500 ml) water (or substitute
  with ruby port for a special treat)
4 C (767 g) sugar
16 C (1.6 kg) whole cranberries

½ t (1 g) of one or more of the
  following: nutmeg, cardamom,
  cinnamon, allspice (optional)
Zest of an orange

1. Follow steps 1 and 2 from the Hot Water Bath Method (see page 28).
2. In a stainless-steel or enamel stockpot, combine orange juice, water or port, and sugar and bring to a boil. Continue boiling for 5 minutes, stirring constantly.
3. Add cranberries and optional spices. Return mixture to a boil. Reduce heat, simmering for another 10 minutes or until berries start to burst. Remove from heat and add orange zest.
4. Using a funnel, pour mixture into hot jars, leaving a ¼-inch (6.4 mm) headspace. Remove any air bubbles with a rubber spatula or skewer.
5. Clean rims and any spills with sterile cloth. Secure lid and screw rings.
6. Place jars on rack in canner with boiling water.
7. Once water returns to a boil, process for 15 minutes, adjusting for altitude if necessary (see page 29).
8. Remove jars and let cool on the counter. Check seal before storing. Refrigerate any unsealed jars and use within 2 weeks.

Locally grown fruits like strawberries are in season for just a few short weeks. Making jam is one of the few ways to enjoy this great flavor all year long.

This section includes recipes for:

Naturally Sweet
  Strawberry Jam
Slow Strawberry Jam
Spiced Blueberry Jam
Peach Jam

Pectin is a substance that occurs naturally in some fruits, such as apples, gooseberries, and many citrus fruits. It enables these fruits to form a jelly or jam consistency. To make other types of jam or jelly, you must add pectin. Most grocery stores sell pectin by the box.

Naturally Sweet
Strawberry Jam

Naturally Sweet Strawberry Jam by Paula Pentel

Makes 5 pints (2.4 l)

Paula Pentel and Callie Wilson once again share one of their fabulous recipes. Standard jam recipes use quite a bit of sugar. This recipe instead creatively uses dried apple pieces, which both sweeten and add pectin, to create the desired jam consistency. Make sure to watch the *Fresh Girl's Guide to Easy Canning and Preserving* DVD to see this great jam made step-by-step.

1 C (90 g) dried apples
2 qts (837 g) strawberries
¼ C (59 ml) lemon juice
1 T (15 ml) pectin mixed with 1 T (12 g) sugar

1. Follow steps 1 and 2 from the Hot Water Bath Method (see page 28).
2. Chop dried apples in food processor.
3. Wash strawberries and remove stems.
4. Add strawberries to a medium-sized, stainless-steel or enamel pan and mash.
5. Add apples and lemon juice to pan. Turn heat to high.
6. Wait until mixture reaches a strong boil, then add pectin-sugar solution.
7. Let cook for 2 minutes or until thickened.
8. Using funnel, pour mixture into hot jars, leaving a ¼-inch (6.4 mm) headspace. Remove any air bubbles with a rubber spatula or clean wooden chopsticks.
9. Clean rims and any spills with sterile cloth. Secure lids and rings.
10. Place jars on rack in canner with boiling water.
11. Once water returns to a boil, process for 5 minutes, adjusting for altitude if necessary (see page 29).
12. Remove jars and let cool on the counter. Check seal before storing. Refrigerate any unsealed jars and use within 2 weeks.

Fruit Jams

Slow Strawberry Jam

Makes 4 pints (1.9 l)

Another method for making low-sugar jam is to slow down the process and let the strawberries thicken on their own time. I call this slow jam and it's one of my favorite recipes. You get the great old-fashioned taste, without overcooking or adding a ton of sugar. You will need a candy thermometer for this recipe.

2 qts (837 g) strawberries
1½ C (288 g) sugar
Juice of a lemon

1. Clean strawberries and remove stems.
2. In a glass or stainless-steel bowl, toss strawberries with sugar and lemon. Cover and let stand for 3–4 hours at room temperature (or 6 hours to overnight in refrigerator).
3. Pour strawberries and juice into a stainless-steel or enamel sauce pan. Bring to a strong simmer for 2 minutes, stirring. Pour mixture back into bowl. Cover and stand 2–3 hours at room temperature (or 6 hours to overnight in refrigerator).
4. Prepare for canning by following steps 1 and 2 from the Hot Water Bath Method (see page 28).
5. Strain liquid from berries. Boil liquid until syrup reaches 220 degrees Fahrenheit on a candy thermometer. Add berries, return to a boil. Mash berries. Reduce to a simmer, simmering for 5–8 minutes until berries are translucent and mixture thickens slightly.
6. Using a funnel, pour mixture into hot jars, leaving a ¼-inch (6.4 mm) headspace. Remove any air bubbles with a rubber spatula or skewer.
7. Clean rims and any spills with sterile cloth. Secure lids and rings.
8. Add to canner and process for 10 minutes, adjusting for altitude if necessary (see page 29).
9. Remove from canner and let cool on the counter. Check seals after 24 hours. Refrigerate any unsealed jars and use within 2 weeks.

Spiced Blueberry Jam

Makes about 5 pints (2.4 l)

24 oz (680 g) blueberries
Packet of powdered pectin
¼ t (518 mg) star anise, ground fine
¼ t (518 mg) ground nutmeg
2 T (30 ml) lemon juice
3 C (575 g) sugar
½ C (125 ml) water

1. Prepare for canning by following steps 1 and 2 from
    the Hot Water Bath Method (see page 28).
2. Wash blueberries and heat them in a stainless-steel or enamel
    saucepan. Add pectin, spices, and lemon juice.
3. Bring mixture to a boil, mash, and return mixture to a gentle boil for 5 minutes.
4. Add sugar and the water; return to a boil for a minute.
5. Using a funnel, pour mixture into hot jars, leaving a ¼-inch (6 mm)
    headspace. Remove any air bubbles with a rubber spatula or skewer.
6. Clean rims and any spills with sterile cloth. Secure lids and rings.
7. Place jars on rack in canner with boiling water.
8. Once water returns to a boil, process for 10 minutes,
    adjusting for altitude if necessary (see page 29).
9. Remove from canner and cool on the counter. After
    24 hours, check seals and store. Refrigerate
    any unsealed jars and use within 2 weeks.

Peach Jam

Makes about 5 pints (2.4 l)

20 medium-sized peaches
¼ C (59 ml) lemon juice
Packet of powdered pectin
5 C (958 g) sugar

1. Prepare for canning by following steps 1 and 2 from the Hot Water Bath Method (see page 28).
2. Prep peaches: Remove skins by dunking peaches into boiling water for 20 seconds. Peel, pit, and cut into slices.
3. Add peaches, lemon juice, and pectin to a stainless-steel or enamel saucepan.
4. Bring to a boil, stirring constantly. Add sugar, return mixture to a boil, and cook for a minute.
5. Using a funnel, pour mixture into hot half-pint or pint (237 or 473 ml) jars, allowing for a ¼-inch (6 mm) headspace. Remove any air bubbles with a rubber spatula or skewer.
6. Clean rims and any spills with sterile cloth. Secure lids and rings.
7. Process for 10 minutes in a boiling water bath. Make sure to adjust for altitude if necessary (see page 29).
8. Remove from canner and cool on the counter. After 24 hours, check seals and store. Refrigerate any unsealed jars and use within 2 weeks.

Variation: To make spiced peach jam, add ground nutmeg and cinnamon to taste (¼ teaspoon [about 600 mg] of each) with the sugar in step 4, or add the zest of an orange.

Tomatoes are a canning favorite for many reasons. They are versatile, plentiful when in season, and lose so much of their flavor and texture when out of season. This section includes recipes that can be processed using a hot water bath. Because tomatoes are less acidic than other fruits, canning recipes that mix tomatoes with certain vegetables and/or meats require a pressure canner. That's why you'll find a recipe for Roasted Tomato Sauce in the pressure canner chapter.

This section includes recipes for:

Tomatoes—whole, halved, and diced
Stewed Tomatoes
Tomato Juice
Tomato Salsa

Salsa

Tomatoes—whole, halved, and diced
Tomatoes, cut into halves or quarters as desired.

3 lbs (1.4 kg) of tomatoes per quart (946 ml). Select tomatoes that are fresh and
   firm, not overripe. Cut into halves, quarters, or smaller chunks as desired.
Salt (optional)
Lemon juice

1. Prepare for canning by following steps 1 and 2 from
    the Hot Water Bath Method (see page 28).
2. Wash and dip tomatoes in boiling water for 30 seconds.
    Plunge into cold water. Drain, peel, and core.
3. Add a teaspoon (5 g) of salt (optional) and 2 tablespoons (30 ml) of
    lemon juice to each sterilized quart jar (for pint [473 ml] jars, add
    ½ teaspoon [3 g] of salt and a tablespoon [15 ml] of lemon juice).
4. Using a funnel, fill jars with tomatoes. Pack tomatoes down
    with a non-metal spoon or spatula. Top off with boiling water,
    leaving a ½-inch (1.3 cm) headspace. Remove any air bubbles
    with a rubber spatula or clean wooden chopstick.
5. Clean rims and any spills with sterile cloth. Secure lids and rings.
6. Place jars in a boiling hot water bath canner.
7. Return water to a boil and process 50 minutes for quarts and
    40 minutes for pints. Adjust for altitude if necessary (see page 29).
8. Remove and let cool on a towel. Check seals after
    24 hours and store. Refrigerate any unsealed
    jars and use within 2 weeks.

Stewed Tomatoes

Makes about 7 quarts (6.6 l)

Stewed tomatoes follow the same procedure as for whole and diced tomatoes except that extra flavor is added through the addition of celery, onions, and green peppers. This makes a great base for many sauces and recipes.

24 C (4 kg) diced tomatoes
2 C (227 g) chopped celery
1 C (151 g) chopped onion
1 C (170 g) chopped green pepper
3 t (5 g) salt

Note: Do not add more onion, celery, or peppers than listed in this recipe unless you are using a pressure canner. It will make the pH balance less acidic and not feasible for hot water bath canning.

1. Prepare for canning by following steps 1 and 2 from the Hot Water Bath Method (see page 28).
2. Combine diced tomatoes and vegetables in a stainless-steel or enamel pot and simmer for 10 minutes.
3. Add a teaspoon (5 g) of salt and 2 tablespoons (30 ml) of lemon juice to each quart (946 ml) (for pint [473 ml] jars, add ½ teaspoon [3 g] of salt and a tablespoon [30 ml] of lemon juice). Pack tomato mix into jars, leaving a ½-inch (1.3 cm) headspace. Remove air bubbles with a non-metal spatula or skewer.
4. Clean rims and any spills with sterile cloth. Secure lids and screw rings.
5. Place jars in a boiling hot water bath canner.
6. Return water to a boil and process 50 minutes for quarts and 40 minutes for pints. Adjust for altitude if necessary (see page 29).
7. Remove and let cool on a towel. Check seals after 24 hours and store. Refrigerate any unsealed jars and use within 2 weeks.

Tomato Juice

Makes about 7 pints (3.3 l)

Fresh, canned tomato and vegetable juice is one of my favorite breakfast treats in the winter. I also keep a jar at my office for a healthy afternoon pick-me-up.

24 C (4 kg) fresh tomatoes, peeled, cored, and diced
2 C (227 g) chopped celery
⅔ C (101 g) chopped onion
3 T (36 g) sugar (to taste)
3 t (15 g) salt
1 t (5 g) black pepper
Tabasco or other hot pepper sauce, to taste
Lemon juice

1. Prepare for canning by following steps 1 and 2 from the Hot Water Bath Method (see page 28).
2. Combine all ingredients in a stainless-steel or enamel pot and simmer, uncovered, for 25 minutes.
3. Force mixture through a food mill or process in a blender and strain through a cheesecloth-lined colander into a bowl.
4. Add 2 tablespoons (30 ml) of lemon juice to each quart jar (for pint [473 ml] jars, add a tablespoon [15 ml] of lemon juice).
5. Using a funnel, fill hot, sterilized jars with tomato juice, leaving a ½-inch (1.3 cm) headspace. Remove any air bubbles with a rubber spatula or skewer.
6. Clean rims and any spills with sterile cloth. Secure lids and rings.
7. Place jars on rack in canner with boiling water.
8. Once water returns to a boil, process 40 minutes for pints and 45 minutes for quarts, adjusting for altitude if necessary (see page 29).
9. Check seals after 24 hours and store. Refrigerate any unsealed jars and use within 2 weeks.

Tomato Salsa

Makes 5 pints (2.4 l)

Check out the bonus chapter of *The Fresh Girl's Guide to Easy Canning and Preserving* DVD to see salsa expert Kathy Hiltsley and her daughter Rachel whip up a great batch of salsa using this recipe!

10 C (1.6 kg) tomatoes, peeled, cored, and diced
1 C (170 g) chopped green pepper
2 C (303 g) chopped onions
½ C (85 g) chopped hot peppers (mixture of banana and jalapeño peppers with seeds removed)

½ C (57 g) celery, finely chopped
5 garlic cloves, chopped
1 T (15 g) salt
2 T (6 g) chopped cilantro
Lemon juice

1. Prepare for canning by following steps 1 and 2 from the Hot Water Bath Method (see page 28).
2. Add diced tomatoes to large, stainless-steel or enamel pot and cook for 30 minutes, until tomatoes are very soft and the large chunks are gone.
3. Using a large spoon or cup, remove excess liquid from the pot, then add remaining ingredients (except lemon juice).
4. Continue to cook at a low boil for 20 minutes, stirring frequently.
5. Using a funnel, fill sterilized canning jars, leaving a ½-inch (1.3 cm) headspace. Add a tablespoon (15 ml) of lemon juice to each jar. Remove any air bubbles with a rubber spatula or skewer.
6. Clean rims and any spills with sterile cloth. Secure lids and screw rings.
7. Process in a hot water bath for 35 minutes, adjusting for altitude if necessary (see page 29).
8. Remove from canner and let cool for 24 hours. Check seal and store. Refrigerate any unsealed jars and use within 2 weeks.

Pickles

Pickling is a great way to put flavor in your pantry and quickly can a lot of fresh vegetables. You can make pickles from cucumbers, beets, beans, peppers, watermelon rinds, and even broccoli stems!

There are two main pickling methods:

1. The first method is quick and easy. Bread and butter pickles, sliced dill, classic sweets, and pickled beets all fall into this category. To make these recipes you simply add a sweet-sour brine of vinegar, sugar, and spices to your selected vegetable and process for 10–15 minutes.

2. The second pickling method involves an extra step. To make dill pickles, sauerkraut, and other tangy and sour pickles, you need to first cure the vegetables by fermenting them for 3–6 weeks. The results are worth the wait!

This chapter will cover:

Bread and Butter Pickles Watermelon Pickles Dill Pickles Quick Dill Pickles Three-Bean Salad

Pickles

Bread and Butter Pickles (also known as classic sweets)

Makes about 7 pints (3.3 l)

25 medium pickling cucumbers, sliced
3 large onions, sliced
½ C (125 g) pickling or canning salt
4 C (1 l) cider vinegar (4–6 percent acidity)
2 C (383 g) sugar
2 t (6 g) turmeric
3 T (28 g) mustard seeds
2 t (5 g) celery seeds

1. Prepare for canning by following steps 1 and 2 from
   the Hot Water Bath Method (see page 28).
2. Combine cucumbers, onions, and salt in a large glass bowl or stainless-
   steel pot and toss to mix. Cover with ice cubes and let stand at room
   temperature for 3 hours. Rinse, drain thoroughly, and set aside.
3. In a large, stainless-steel or enamel saucepan, combine vinegar, sugar, and
   spices. Bring to a boil. Add cucumber and onion mix. Return to a boil.
4. Ladle vegetables into hot, sterilized jars. Make sure the brine
   fully covers the pickles. Leave a ½-inch (1.3 cm) headspace.
   Remove any air bubbles with a rubber spatula or skewer.
5. Clean rims and any spills with sterile cloth. Secure lids and rings.
6. Process for 10 minutes, adjusting for altitude if necessary (see
   page 29). Pickles will stay crisper if you can maintain a water
   temperature between 200 and 205 degrees Fahrenheit during
   processing. Use a candy thermometer to monitor.
7. Remove from canner and let cool on the counter. Check seals after 24 hours
   and store. Refrigerate any unsealed jars and use within 2 weeks.

Watermelon Pickles

Makes 4–5 pints (1.9–2.4 l)

An old-fashioned, thrifty treat! Thanks to the University of Minnesota Extension office for the great recipe.

½ large watermelon
¾ C (180 g) canning salt
3 qts (2.8 l) water
2 trays ice cubes
1 T (about 48) (6 g) whole cloves
6 1-inch (2.5 cm) pieces stick cinnamon
8 C (1.5 kg) sugar
3 C (750 ml) white vinegar (4–6 percent acidity)
3 C (750 ml) water
Lemon, thinly sliced and seeded

1. Prepare for canning by following steps 1 and 2 from the Hot Water Bath Method (see page 28).
2. Cut rind and all pink edges from the watermelon. Remove dark green peel. Cut into 1-inch (2.5 cm) squares. Toss into a stockpot.
3. Mix salt with 3 quarts (2.8 l) of water. Pour over watermelon rinds. Add ice cubes. Let stand for 5–6 hours. Drain and rinse.
4. Cover rinds with cold water and cook until fork tender, about 10 minutes. Drain.
5. Tie spices into a spice packet by securing in a clean piece of cheesecloth.
6. Combine sugar, vinegar, 3 cups (750 ml) of water, and spice packet in a stainless-steel or enamel saucepan. Boil for 5 minutes and pour over the watermelon (keep the spice packet in); add lemon slices.
7. Cover and let stand overnight.
8. Heat watermelon in syrup to boiling and cook until translucent, about 10 minutes.

9. Using a funnel, pack rinds into hot, sterilized, pint (473 ml) jars. To each jar add a piece of stick cinnamon from the spice bag. Cover with boiling syrup, leaving a ½-inch (1.3 cm) headspace. Remove any air bubbles with a rubber spatula or skewer.

10. Clean rims and any spills with sterile cloth. Secure lids and screw rings.

11. Process in simmering water bath at 200 to 205 degrees Fahrenheit for 5 minutes, adjusting for altitude if necessary (see page 29). Use a candy thermometer to maintain optimal water temperature. (Pickles will stay crisper if you are able to maintain a temperature between 200 and 205 degrees Fahrenheit, just below a full boil. If you don't have a candy thermometer, or are unable to maintain this temperature, your pickles will still be fine, just a little softer.)

12. Remove jars from canner. Cool for 24 hours, test seals, and store. Refrigerate any unsealed jars and use within 2 weeks.

Pickling Tips:

* Use freshly picked, firm vegetables.
* If your water is hard, boil water you'll be using in recipes for 15 minutes. Decant into another container, leaving any sediment behind.
* Use additive-free salt (canning, pickling, and kosher salt work well). Regular table salt has additives to prevent caking.
* Use whole, fresh spices. Older spices can impart a bitter taste.
* Follow recipes' ratios of salt, sugar, and acidity.
* Check the label of your vinegar to ensure the acidity level is between 4 and 6 percent.

Dill Pickles

Makes about 5–6 quarts (4.7–5.7 l)

These pickles rely on fermentation to produce the earthy, complex flavor loved for centuries. Fermenting pickles is a simple procedure, but it does require 3–6 weeks. In addition to the regular canning equipment, you'll need a container—a stone crock, glass container, or food-grade plastic container all work. You could also use a 5-gallon (19 l) container for this recipe if you desired. You'll also need a plate or glass pie pan that fits inside your container, leaving just a bit of room at the edges. As with all food preservation, make sure all containers are clean and sterilized.

10 lbs (4.5 kg) pickling cucumbers, 3–4 inches long
3 bunches fresh dill
1 ½ C (375 g) canning or pickling salt
1 C (250 ml) vinegar (4–6 percent acidity)
5 garlic cloves
½ C (125 g) pickling spice*
20 C (4.7 l) water

Tip: To make your own pickling spice, combine a cinnamon stick broken into pieces, 3 crushed bay leaves, 2 tablespoons (19 g) of mustard seeds, 2 tablespoons (3 g) of coriander seeds, a teaspoon of whole cloves (2 g), a teaspoon (542 mg) of fennel seeds, and a tablespoon (8 g) of peppercorns.

To Ferment
1. Wash cucumbers. Cut ¹⁄₁₆-inch (2 mm) slices off blossom ends and trim stems, leaving ¼ inch (6 mm) of stem attached. Place half of dill and spices on bottom of your stone, glass, or food-grade plastic container.
2. Add cucumbers, remaining dill, and spices. Dissolve salt in vinegar and water and pour over cucumbers.

3. Cover with plate or glass pie pan. Place 2–3 quart-sized (946 ml) canning jars filled with water and secured with lids on top of plate. Make sure cucumbers are always covered with 1–2 inches (2.5–5 cm) of brine.
4. Store where temperature is between 70 and 75 degrees Fahrenheit for 3–4 weeks to allow pickles to ferment. Temperatures of 60 to 70 degrees Fahrenheit are acceptable, but the fermentation will take 5 to 6 weeks. At temperatures above 80 degrees Fahrenheit, your pickles will spoil.
5. Check the container several times a week and promptly remove surface scum or mold. *If the pickles become soft, slimy, or develop a disagreeable odor, discard them.* Cucumbers are ready when they turn a translucent olive green color. Taste them to check!

To Can
6. Prepare for canning by following steps 1 and 2 from the Hot Water Bath Method (see page 28).
7. Remove the pickles from the brine. Pour the brine into a stockpot. Heat to a boil and simmer 5 minutes. Filter through paper coffee filters into a bowl or pot.
8. Using a funnel, fill hot, sterilized jar with pickles and cover with hot brine, leaving a ½-inch (1.3cm) headspace. Remove any air bubbles with a rubber spatula or skewer.
9. Process pints (473 ml) for 15 minutes, quarts (946 ml) for 20 minutes, adjusting for altitude if necessary (see page 29).
10. Remove jars from canner. Cool for 24 hours, test seals, and store. Refrigerate any unsealed jars and use within 2 weeks.

Quick Dill Pickles

Makes about 7 quarts (6.6 l)

14 lbs (6.4 kg) pickling cucumbers, 2–3 inches (5–7.5 cm) long
7 fresh dill heads (or 4 T [57 g] finely chopped dill weed)
7 onion slices, ½-inch (1.3 cm) thick
14 garlic cloves
7 t (22 g) mustard seeds
12 C (2.8 l) water
4 C (946 ml) white vinegar (4–6 percent acidity)
½ C sugar
⅔ C (160 g) canning or pickling salt

1. Prepare for canning by following steps 1 and 2 from
   the Hot Water Bath Method (see page 28).
2. Wash and scrub the cucumbers. Remove blossom end, leaving
   ¼ inch (6 mm) of the stem attached, if possible.
3. Combine water, vinegar, sugar, and salt in a stainless-steel or
   enamel pot and bring to a boil.
4. Place two garlic cloves, a slice of onion, a dill head (or
   1 ½ teaspoon [7 g] of chopped dill weed) and a teaspoon (3 g)
   of mustard seeds into the bottom of a quart-sized (about a liter)
   canning jar (for pint [473 g] jars, halve these quantities).
5. Put the cucumbers into hot, sterilized jars. Cover cucumbers
   with boiling hot brine, leaving a ½-inch (1.3 cm) headspace.
   Remove any air bubbles with a rubber spatula or skewer.
6. Process jars in simmering water bath at 200 to 205 degrees Fahrenheit
   for 10 minutes, adjusting for altitude if necessary (see page 29).
7. Remove jars from canner. Cool for 24 hours, test seals, and store.
   Refrigerate any unsealed jars and use within 2 weeks.

Three-Bean Salad

Makes 5 half-pints (1.2 l)

This is a classic American salad. Just as great to eat at a July
Fourth picnic or with Thanksgiving leftovers!

1 ½ C (194 g) green beans
1 ½ C (194 g) yellow beans
½ C (125 ml) white vinegar
  (4–6 percent acidity)
¼ C (59 ml) bottled lemon juice
¾ C (144 g) sugar
1 ¼ C (296 ml) water

¼ C (60 ml) oil
½ t (3 g) canning or pickling salt
1 C (164 g) canned, drained
  garbanzo beans
Medium onion, thinly sliced
1 ½ stalks celery, thinly sliced
½ medium green pepper, diced

1. Prepare for canning by following steps 1 and 2 from
   the Hot Water Bath Method (see page 28).
2. Cut beans into 1 ½-inch (4 cm) pieces. Blanch 3 minutes
   in boiling water. Cool in an ice water bath.
3. Combine vinegar, lemon juice, sugar, and water in a stainless-steel or
   enamel stockpot and bring to a boil. Remove from heat. Add oil and salt
   and mix well. Add beans, onions, celery, and green pepper to solution
   and bring to a simmer. Turn off heat and cool to room temperature.
4. Marinate 12 to 14 hours in refrigerator.
5. Return mixture to medium high heat and bring to a boil.
6. Ladle into clean, sterilized jars, leaving a ½-inch (1.3 cm) headspace.
   Remove any air bubbles with a rubber spatula or skewer.
7. Clean rims and any spills with sterile cloth. Secure lids and screw rings.
8. Process in a hot water bath for 20 minutes, adjusting
   for altitude if necessary (see page 29).
9. Remove from canner. Let cool for 24 hours, test seals, and store.
   Refrigerate any unsealed jars and use within 2 weeks.

Pressure Canning

In this chapter you'll find recipes requiring a pressure canner. Vegetables and other foods with low pH values need to be processed in a pressure canner for safe preservation. Using a pressure canner is very simple and rewards you with great food and delicious meals. Make sure to watch the pressure canner segments of *The Fresh Girl's Guide to Easy Canning and Preserving* DVD for detailed instructions.

This chapter will cover:

Whole and Diced Vegetables

Stocks & Soups

A pressure canner is simply a large pot with a lid that seals, creating air pressure inside the canner. The lid has a rubber ring inside the rim and an interlocking lid to create a seal when twisted shut. This allows you to process food at a higher temperature, 240 degrees Fahrenheit. As we've mentioned elsewhere in the book, all low-acid foods (vegetables, meats, and beans, for example) must be processed at this higher temperature to sterilize and safely preserve the food.

Pressure canner lids have several important elements:
* **Safety valve.** This rubber stopper pops out if too much pressure builds in the canner.
* **Vent pipe.** Steam building up in the canner is released and regulated through a vent pipe on top of the canner lid.
* **Regulator or weight.** Once steam has built and is being released from the vent pipe, a regulator or weight (depending on your canner model) is placed on top of the vent pipe to stop or slow the release of steam and build pressure in the canner.
* **Dial gauge.** Some canners come with a numbered dial gauge to monitor pressure level.

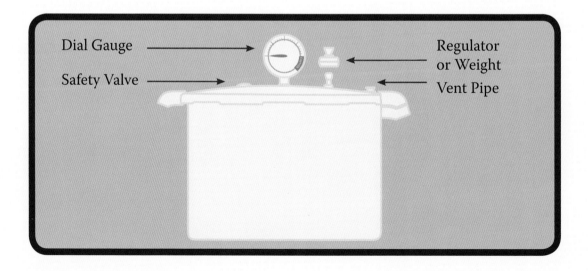

Purchasing a Pressure Canner

It's best to purchase your canner new and to stick to the main brands: All-American, Mirro, and Presto. These producers are still in business, have extra parts, and offer support services. Old canners aren't as safe as the newer models. They're often made of aluminum, which warps easily, and don't have as many safety features as today's modern pressure canners.

Always make sure the parts of your canner are in good shape. You can have your canner tested periodically by your local Extension Service.

Type: Pressure canners either use a numbered dial for pressure readings or regulator weights to monitor the amount of pressure. The dial displays readings from 0 to 25 pounds of pressure. You monitor the dial reading to establish the correct pressure level for your recipe. Weighted gauge canners uses weights, which create 5, 10, or 15 pounds of pressure inside the canner when they are placed on top of the vent pipe. Both styles work well for canning. I have both types and prefer the dial gauge for the simple fact that I like to watch the pressure rise and know where it is during processing. Dial gauge canners are better for canning at higher altitudes, where you need to increase the pressure in 1-pound increments based on your altitude level.

Size: A 16-quart (15.1 l) canner is sufficient for most folks. It holds 7 quart jars (946.4 ml), or 10 pint jars (473.2 ml). If you plan to can in large quantities, the larger 22- or 23-quart-sized (20.8 or 21.8 l) canners hold 7 quart jars (946.4 ml) jars, but allow you to stack two layers of pint jars (473.2 ml) for processing.

Pressure Canners cost between $80 and $250, depending on type and size. I recommend the Presto brand. It is affordable, durable, and has an easy-to-read dial pressure gauge.

Pressure Canning Method

Follow these steps for safe and easy pressure canning at home!

1. Follow the sterilization instructions on page 18.

2. Prepare your canning recipe, using only recipes meant for home canning. Fill your sterilized jars with the food, leaving the amount of headspace called for in your recipe. Use a nonreactive kitchen utensil, such as a narrow rubber spatula or a bamboo skewer, to remove air bubbles. Air bubbles can cause uneven heating during processing and may impair the jar's ability to seal. Using a clean towel or paper towel, wipe the rims of the jars. This removes any spilled liquid or food, which can also prevent the jar from sealing. Place a dome lid on top of the jar and secure with a jar ring, screwing on so it's secure but not tight.

3. ALWAYS place jars on a rack to submerge jars into the canner. Jars that come into contact with direct heat through the bottom of the canning pot can crack and break. Add several inches (about eight centimeters) of water to the canner. Add a splash of vinegar to keep your jars free of mineral deposits. Close the canner lid securely. Turn the burner to high.

4. Bring the water to a boil. Allow the steam to escape from the top of the pot for ten minutes. Place a weight or a gauge on the canner at this point.

5. Start timing once the canner achieves the desired pressure level. With a dial gauge, you can see the pressure level. With weighted pressure canner models, the regulator weights will start rocking. Do read the directions that come with your model of canner. Once you've reached the proper pressure level, turn down the heat a bit to maintain consistent pressure. When the pressure level varies too much, the contents of your canning jars can spill out. Keep a close eye on your canner. This is not the time to run errands or take a nap!

6. Once the processing time has elapsed, turn off the heat. Allow the pressure to return to zero. Then open the vent to release any excess steam. Open the lid and use the jar lifter to remove the jars. Place them on a towel on your countertop and let them rest until cooled. After twenty-four hours, test the seals by pressing slightly on the center of the dome lid. If the lid makes a hollow popping sound and moves up and down, it isn't sealed. When this happens, refrigerate the jar and eat the contents within two weeks. Be sure to label canned foods with the recipe name and date the item was canned. Store in a cool, dry place. Eat within one year.

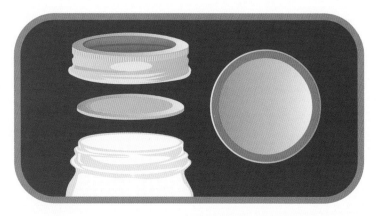

1 Sterilize equipment and cooking area.

2 Prepare recipe. Fill jars, leaving proper headspace. Remove air bubbles. Wipe rims, seal.

3 Place jars in canner on rack. Add several inches (about 8 cm) of water to canner. Close canner lid. Turn burner to high.

4 Bring water to boil, allowing steam to escape for 10 minutes. Place weight or gauge on canner.

5 Heat canner until pressure achieves desired level. Reduce heat to hold pressure for required time (hold pressure steady).

6 Turn off heat. Allow pressure to return to zero. Open vent, releasing excess steam. Open lid. Remove jars. Cool jars for 24 hours, test seals. Refrigerate any unsealed jars and use within 2 weeks.

Adjust for Your Altitude

Before you start, visit www.EarthTools.org to determine your altitude.

There are two types of pressure canners: dial gauge (where a gauge displays the pressure reading) and weighted gauge. Follow the guide below to adjust the pressure in your canner. Also, be sure to read your canner's instruction manual.

Dial gauge pressure canner:
    * For altitudes up to 2,000 feet (610 m), process jars at 11 pounds of pressure.
    * For altitudes between 2,000 and 4,000 feet (610 m and 1.2 km),
      process at 12 pounds of pressure.
    * For altitudes between 4,000 and 6,000 feet (1.2 and 1.8 km)
      process at 13 pounds of pressure.
    * For altitudes between 6,000 and 8,000 feet (1.8 and 2.4 km)
      process at 14 pounds of pressure.

Weighted gauge pressure canner:
    * For altitudes up to 1,000 feet above sea level,
      cook using the 10 pounds of pressure regulator.
    * For altitudes greater than 1,000 feet, cook using
      the 15 pound weighted regulator.

Home canning is a great way to enjoy summer vegetables and make quick meals. My favorite veggies to can are beets, beans, and succotash made from corn and lima beans. I also can a lot of cubed winter squash, which makes great soups and squash risotto!

There are a number of vegetables that are not recommended for home canning. Broccoli and cauliflower become discolored and their strong flavors are unpleasantly intensified. Summer squash, zucchini, cabbage, and eggplant become mushy and off-flavored as well.

This chapter will cover:

Asparagus
Beans, Green & Wax
Beans, Lima
Beets
Carrots
Corn
Peas, Shelled
　　　Peppers
　　　Potatoes
　　　Squash & Pumpkin

Potatoes

Asparagus

24 pounds (11 kg) of asparagus
will yield 7 quarts (6.6 l)

Wash and trim so spears can stand up in
your jars. Pack into hot, sterilized jars. Add
a teaspoon (5 g) of salt (optional). Fill jars
with boiling water, making sure asparagus
is fully submerged. Leave a 1-inch (2.5 cm)
of headspace. Follow canning steps
3–6 of the Pressure Canning Method
on pages 60–61. Process pints (473 ml)
for 30 minutes and quarts (946 ml) for
40 minutes in canner at pressure listed for
your altitude and canner (see page 64).

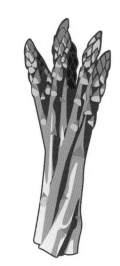

Beans, Green & Wax

14 pounds (6.4 kg) of beans will yield
approximately 7 quarts (6.6 l)

Wash and trim ends. Snap into smaller
pieces if desired. Pack into hot, sterilized
jars. Add a teaspoon (5 g) of salt (optional).
Fill jars with boiling water, covering
beans. Leave a 1-inch (2.5 cm) headspace.
Follow canning steps 3–6 of the Pressure
Canning Method on pages 60–61. Process
pints (473 ml) and quarts (946 ml) for
25 minutes in canner at pressure listed for
your altitude and canner (see page 64).

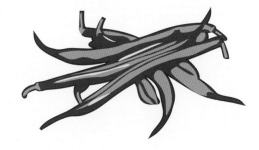

Beans, Lima

30 pounds (13.6 kg) of lima beans will yield approximately 7 quarts (6.6 l)

Wash and shell. Pack into hot, sterilized jars. Add a teaspoon (5 g) of salt (optional). Fill jars with boiling water, covering beans. Leave a 1-inch (2.5 cm) headspace. Follow canning steps 3–6 of the Pressure Canning Method on pages 60–61. Process pints (473 ml) for 40 minutes and quarts (946 ml) for 50 minutes at pressure listed for your altitude and canner (see page 64).

Beets

21 pounds (9.5 kg) of beets yields approximately 7 quarts (6.6 l)

Wash and boil for 20 minutes. Remove skins. Cut into cubes. Pack into hot, sterilized jars. Add a teaspoon (5 g) of salt (optional). Fill jars with boiling water, covering beets. Leave a 1-inch (2.5 cm) headspace. Follow canning steps 3–6 of the Pressure Canning Method on pages 60–61. Process pints (473 ml) for 30 minutes and quarts (946 ml) for 35 minutes at pressure listed for your altitude and canner (see page 64).

Carrots

20 pounds (9 kg) of carrots yields
approximately 7 quarts (6.6 l)

Wash, peel, and slice to desired size. Pack into hot,
sterilized jars. Add a teaspoon (5 g) of salt (optional).
Fill jars with boiling water, covering carrots. Leave
a 1-inch (2.5 cm) headspace. Follow canning steps
3–6 of the Pressure Canning Method on pages
60–61. Process pints (473 ml) for 25 minutes and
quarts (946 ml) for 30 minutes at pressure listed
for your altitude and canner (see page 64).

Corn

30 pounds (13.6 kg) of corn (on the cob) will
yield approximately 7 quarts (6.6 l)

Husk, cook in boiling water for 3 minutes, cut
corn off cobs. Pack into hot, sterilized jars. Add
a teaspoon (5 g) of salt (optional). Fill jars with
boiling water, covering corn. Leave a 1-inch
(2.5 cm) headspace. Follow canning steps 3–6 of
the Pressure Canning Method on pages 60–
61. Process pints (473 ml) for 25 minutes and
quarts (946 ml) for 30 minutes at pressure listed
for your altitude and canner (see page 64).

Peas, Shelled

20 pounds (9 kg) of peas will yield 9 pints (4.3 l)

Wash peas. Fill jars with raw peas. Add a teaspoon (5 g) of salt (optional). Fill jars with boiling water, covering peas. Leave a 1-inch (2.5 cm) headspace. Secure lids. Follow canning instructions on page 60–61. Process pints (473 ml) and quarts (946 ml) for 40 minutes at pressure listed above for your altitude and canner (see page 64).

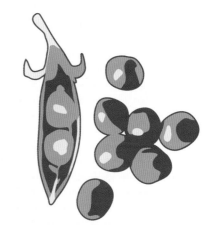

Peppers

10 pounds (4.5 kg) of peppers will yield 9 pints (4.3 l)

Blanch peppers in boiling water or blister in a broiler for 6 minutes. Place in a bowl and cover with plastic wrap or a tight-fitting plate. Let sit until cool and then remove skins. Cut to desired size. Fill hot, sterilized jars with peppers. Add a ½ teaspoon (2.5 g) of salt (optional). Fill jars with boiling water, covering peppers. Leave a 1-inch (2.5 cm) headspace. Follow canning steps 3–6 of the Pressure Canning Method on pages 60–61. Process pints (473 ml) for 35 minutes at pressure listed for your altitude and canner (see page 64).

Whole and Diced Vegetables

Potatoes

20 pounds (9.1 kg) of potatoes will yield 7 quarts (6.6 l)

Wash and peel potatoes. Cut into ½- or 1-inch (1.3 or 2.5 cm) cubes. Important: To prevent them from darkening, place the cubed potatoes in water with an ascorbic acid solution. The easiest way to do this is to crush six 500 mg Vitamin C tablets per gallon of water (see the tip on preventing discoloration on page 35). Keep the potatoes submerged until you are ready to cook them. Otherwise, they'll turn a very unappetizing color of gray when canned and stored. Transfer potatoes to boiling water and cook for 2 minutes. Fill hot, sterilized jars with hot potatoes. Add a teaspoon (5 g) of salt (optional). Fill jars with fresh boiling water, covering potatoes. Leave a 1-inch (2.5 cm) headspace. Follow canning steps 3–6 of the Pressure Canning Method on pages 60–61. Process pints (473 ml) for 35 minutes and quarts (946 ml) for 40 minutes at pressure listed for your altitude and canner (see page 64).

Squash (winter) and Pumpkin:

18 pounds (8 kg) of squash or pumpkin
will yield approximately 7 quarts (6.6 l)

Select winter squash and pumpkins with a hard
rind. Do not use spaghetti squash or other
varieties with stringy pulp. Smaller pumpkins
meant for pies (as opposed to ones used for
carving Jack-o-lanterns) produce better results.
Wash squash, remove seeds, peel, and cut into
1-inch (2.5 cm) pieces. Cook squash in boiling
water for 2 minutes. Pack jars with cubes of
squash/pumpkin. Fill jars with boiling water,
covering squash. Leave a 1-inch (2.5 cm)
headspace. Follow canning steps 3–6 of the
Pressure Canning Method on pages 60–61.
Process pints (473 ml) for 55 minutes and
quarts (946 ml) for 90 minutes at pressure listed
for your altitude and canner (see page 64).

Note: Do not mash or puree squash prior to
canning; the puree is too dense to reliably heat
through. Keep the squash/pumpkin cubes intact
for safe canning. To make purees or soups
later, simply dump the canned squash cubes
into a blender and mix for a few minutes.

Stocks and Soups

Stocks and soups fill my pantry. They're great for saving lots of money and getting fast, healthy meals on the table in minutes. This section provides recipes for some of the basics. Later on, I'll show you soups with more variations and different flavors.

This section will cover:

Chicken or Beef Stock
Vegetable Stock
Chicken Soup
Creamy Squash Soup
Roasted Tomato Sauce

Chicken Br

Roasted
Spaghetti Sauce

Creamy
Squash Soup

Chicken or Beef Stock

Makes 6 pints or 3 quarts (2.8 l)

3 lbs (1.4 kg) of chicken pieces or 6 lbs (2.7 kg) meaty beef bones
3 qts (2.8 l) water
2 stalks celery, diced
2 onions, quartered
2 leeks (optional, but adds a nice flavor)
4 garlic cloves, chopped
12 black peppercorns
2 bay leaves
1 ½ T (7.5 g) salt

1. In a large stainless-steel or enamel pot, combine all ingredients. Bring to a boil, then reduce heat and simmer for 2 ½ hours.
2. Sterilize jars, lids, and utensils.
3. Remove chicken pieces or beef bones (reserve chicken for another use) and strain stock through a colander or sieve lined with cheesecloth.
4. Let cool and skim fat.
5. Return stock to a boil.
6. Ladle stock into hot, sterilized jars. Leave a 1-inch (2.5 cm) headspace. Secure lids.
7. Follow canning steps 3–6 of the Pressure Canning Method (see pages 60–61). Process pints (473 ml) for 20 minutes and quarts (946 ml) for 25 minutes at pressure listed for your altitude and canner (see page 64).
8. Remove jars from the canner. Let cool for 24 hours, test seals, and store. Store any unsealed cans in the refrigerator and consume within 2 weeks.

Vegetable Stock

Makes 8 pints or 4 quarts (3.8 l)

3 qts (2.8 l) water
1 lb (453 g) carrots
4 stalks celery
2 onions
½ lb (227 g) mushrooms
1 red bell pepper

4 garlic cloves, sliced
3 bay leaves
1 t (542 mg) dried thyme
12 whole peppercorns
½ lb (227 g) shallots (optional)
Other herbs as desired for more flavor

1. Chop vegetables (can be larger pieces).
2. In a large stainless-steel or enamel pot, combine all ingredients. Bring to a boil, then reduce heat and simmer for 2 ½ hours. Uncover and continue to simmer for an additional hour.
3. Sterilize jars, lids, and utensils.
4. Strain stock through a colander or sieve lined with cheesecloth.
5. Let cool and skim fat.
6. Return stock to a boil.
7. Ladle stock into hot jars. Leave a 1-inch (2.5 cm) headspace. Secure lids.
8. Follow canning steps 3–6 of the Pressure Canning Method (see pages 60–61). Process pints (473 ml) for 30 minutes or quarts (946 ml) for 35 minutes at pressure listed for your altitude and canner (see page 64).
9. Remove jars from the canner. Let cool for 24 hours, test seals, and store. Store any unsealed cans in the refrigerator and consume within 2 weeks.

Chicken Soup

Makes 6 pints or 3 quarts (2.8 l)

2 C (907 g) diced chicken
3 qts (2.8 l) chicken stock (see recipe for Chicken Stock on page 73)
2 stalks celery, diced
3 carrots, diced
1 large onion, diced
1 t (542 mg) dried tarragon (or other herb if preferred)
1 T (15 g) salt
1 t (5 g) freshly ground pepper

1. In a large stainless-steel or enamel pot, combine all ingredients.
   Bring to a boil, then reduce heat and simmer for 30 minutes.
2. Sterilize jars, lids, and utensils.
3. Ladle soup into hot jars. Leave a 1-inch (2.5 cm) headspace. Secure lids.
4. Follow canning steps 3–6 of the Pressure Canning Method (see pages
   60–61). Process pints (473 ml) for 75 minutes or quarts (946 ml) for
   90 minutes at pressure listed for your altitude and canner (see page 64).
5. Remove jars from the canner. Let cool for 24 hours, test seals, and store.
   Store any unsealed cans in the refrigerator and consume within 2 weeks.

Note: Do NOT can chicken soup with noodles. When you're ready
to eat chicken noodle soup, pour canned broth and vegetables into
a pan and add the noodles. Cook until noodles are tender.

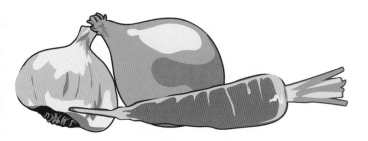

Creamy Squash Soup

Makes about 5 quarts (4.7 l)

5 celery stalks, cut into ½-inch (1.3 cm) cubes
5 carrots, cut into ½-inch (1.3 cm) cubes
3 onions, chopped
2 ½ lbs (1 kg) potatoes (red or other boiling potatoes)
5 lbs (2.3 kg) butternut squash, peeled and cut into ½-inch (1.3 cm) cubes
2 T (30 g) salt
Boiling water

1. Sterilize jars, lids, and equipment.
2. Peel and cut potatoes into ½-inch (1.3 cm) cubes. To prevent darkening, soak in an ascorbic acid solution of three 500 mg Vitamin C tablets crushed into 2 quarts (1.9 l) of water.
3. Boil squash and potato cubes for two minutes.
4. Pack squash, potatoes, onions, carrots, and celery into jars. Do not mash!
5. Cover with boiling water, leaving a 1-inch (2.5 cm) headspace.
6. Follow canning steps 3–6 of the Pressure Canning Method on pages 60–61. Process pints (473 ml) for 55 minutes and quarts (946 ml) for 90 minutes at pressure listed for your altitude and canner (see page 64).
7. When you're ready to eat, drain squash/potato mixture. Add it to a blender with a cup (250 ml) of milk, cream, or water per quart (946 ml) of canned vegetables (more or less, depending on how thick you like your soup). Pour into a pan and heat. Add additional spices at this time according to your taste. Curry or ginger adds great flavor.

Roasted Tomato Sauce

Makes approximately 5 quarts (4.7 l)

This is a staple in my pantry. It's great for a quick pasta meal, as a chili base, and in lasagna. It's processed in a pressure canner because this recipe calls for meat.

15 lbs (6.8 kg) tomatoes, halved
  (about 75 medium Roma tomatoes
  are the best for canning)
3 beets, diced or ¼ C (30 g) sugar
12 garlic cloves, halved
1 t (5 ml) olive oil
2 T (52 g) dried basil

2 T (52 g) dried oregano
2 t (10 g) salt
Pepper to taste
2 onions, chopped
1 ½ lbs (680 g) ground pork
  sausage, beef, or combination

1. Preheat oven to 350 degrees Fahrenheit.
2. Place halved tomatoes, beets (if using—they add a nice, natural sweetness to the sauce), and garlic in a large roasting pan (3-inch [7.5 cm] or higher sides). You may need to roast in shifts. Sprinkle with herbs, salt, and pepper. Roast for 60 minutes.
3. Sterilize jars, lids, and utensils.
4. Let tomatoes and beets cool. Remove skins and seeds—the skins pull off easily and I give each tomato a squeeze to remove the seeds. Lightly puree in blender.
5. Heat olive oil in a large stainless-steel or enamel pot, add onions, and sauté for 5 minutes. Add ground beef and/or sausage and cook for 10 minutes until browned.
6. Add tomato mixture to meat, bring to a boil, reduce to a simmer, and cook for 20 minutes. If using sugar, add during this step.
7. Ladle into hot, sterilized jars, leaving a 1-inch (2.5 cm) headspace. Secure lids.
8. Follow canning steps 3–6 of the Pressure Canning Method on pages 60–61. Process pints (473 ml) for 60 minutes or quarts (946 l) for 70 minutes at pressure listed for your altitude and canner (see page 64).
9. Remove jars from the canner. Let cool for 24 hours, test seals, and store. Store any unsealed cans in the refrigerator and consume within 2 weeks.

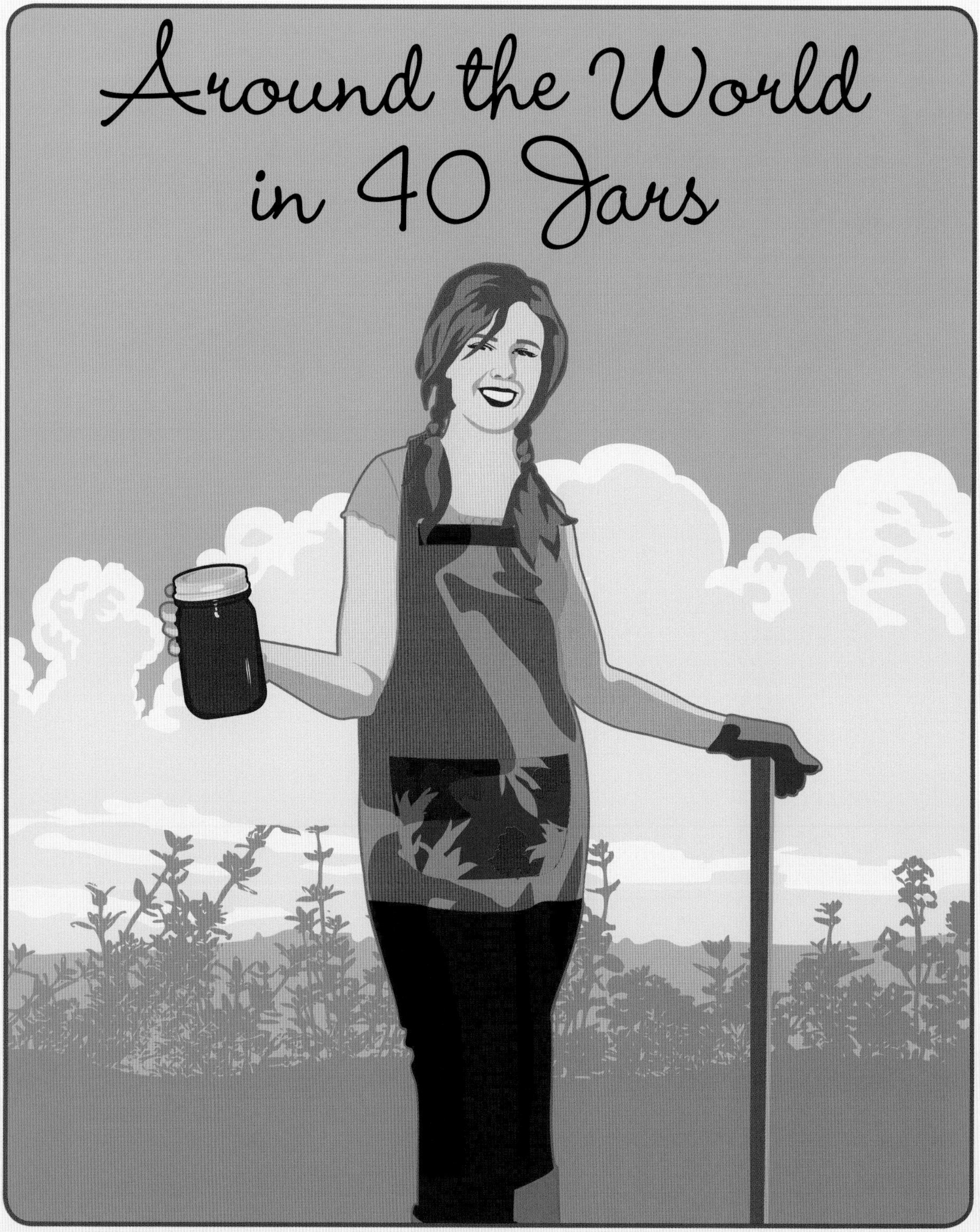
Around the World
in 40 Jars

Let's Can!...Foods From Around the World

It's easy to add some flavor and fun to your canning. The next forty recipes draw on flavor combinations and favorites dishes from cultures around the globe.

This section will cover:

Appetizers
Soups and Stews
Main Dishes
Side Dishes
Desserts
Sauces and Condiments

Minestrone

Bruschetta, Italy

Makes 5 half-pints (1 l)
Method: Hot Water Bath

5 lbs (2.3 kg) tomatoes (plum are best), halved
6 garlic cloves, minced
½ C (45 g) sundried tomatoes (purchase dried, not soaked-in oil)
3 T (45 ml) balsamic vinegar
3 T (5 g) dried basil
1 T (15 g) salt
½ t (2.5 g) ground pepper
½ C (118 ml) red wine

1. Follow canning preparation and processing instructions
   for the Hot Water Bath Method (see page 28).
2. Roast tomatoes and garlic by laying them in a single layer on a baking
   sheet and cooking 2 inches (5 cm) from the heating unit with the oven set
   to broil. Broil for 10–12 minutes, until the tomatoes skin start to char.
3. Let tomatoes cool for a few minutes. Remove skins and seeds. Chop.
4. Reconstitute sundried tomatoes by soaking them in
   boiling water for 5 minutes. Drain and mince.
5. Combine all ingredients in a stockpot. Bring to a boil.
   Reduce heat, cover, and simmer for 10 minutes.
6. Pack mix into hot, sterilized jars, leaving a ½-inch (1.3 cm) headspace.
   Remove air bubbles. Wipe rims and secure lids.
7. Process half-pints (237 ml) and pints (473 ml) for 20 minutes in a
   hot water bath, adjusting for altitude if necessary (see page 29).
8. To serve, cut a baguette into ¾-inch (1.9 cm) slices. Arrange on a baking
   sheet and broil for 1–2 minutes. Spoon tomato mixture over the top. Sprinkle
   with shredded Parmesan or mozzarella cheese. Broil for 5 minutes.

Pickled Pepperoncini, Italy

Makes 5 pints (2.4 l)
Method: Hot Water Bath

These pickled peppers add a great splash of taste to sandwiches
or as an appetizer with cheeses and cured meats.

30 medium-sized peppers (pepperoncini, hot banana, or Tuscan all work well)
1 ½ C (362 g) canning or pickling salt
1 g (3.8 l) plus 2 C (474 ml) water, divided
7 C (1.7 l) white vinegar (4–6 percent acidity)
1 C (192 g) sugar
5 garlic cloves

1. Wash peppers. Leave up to an inch (2.5 cm) of stem on each
    pepper. Cut two small slits in each pepper (wear plastic gloves
    to prevent hot pepper oils from getting onto your hands).
2. In a large glass or food-grade plastic container, dissolve salt
    in a gallon (3.8 l) of water. Add peppers. Cover with a dinner
    plate to hold peppers below water. Weight the plate with a
    sealed glass jar filled with water. Let set for 12–18 hours.
3. Follow canning preparation and processing instructions
    from the Hot Water Bath Method (see page 28).
4. Drain and rinse peppers well.
5. Bring 2 cups (474 ml) of water, vinegar, and sugar to a boil.
    Simmer for 15 minutes.
6. Add a clove of garlic to each jar. Pack peppers into hot, sterilized jars. Fill jars
    with hot liquid, covering peppers. Leave a ½-inch (1.3 cm) headspace. Wipe
    rims and secure lids.
7. Process pints (473 ml) for 10 minutes, quarts (946 ml) for 15 minutes
    in a hot water bath, adjusting for altitude if necessary (see page 29).

Salsa Verde, Mexico

Makes 5 pints (2.4 l)
Method: Hot Water Bath

2 medium poblano peppers (or
   other mild, green chili peppers)
½ C (256 g) jalapeño peppers
5 C (804 g) tomatillos,
   husked and chopped
3 C (483 g) chopped onions
½ C (118 ml) lemon juice

½ C (118 ml) lime juice
½ C (118 ml) white distilled vinegar
6 garlic cloves, finely chopped
1 T (2 g) ground cumin
2 T (3 g) cilantro
1 T (15 g) salt
½ t (271 mg) cayenne pepper

Note: Do not add more onion or peppers than listed in this recipe unless you
are using the pressure canner. These are low-acid vegetables and will reduce
the acidity of the overall recipe to a level unsafe for hot water bath canning. The
added vinegar is also important to this and all salsa recipes for home canning.
Vinegar increases the overall acidity of salsa recipes to ensure safe canning.

1. Roast peppers under a broiler, turning every few minutes to char skin.
    Dunk into ice water. Remove skins and seeds and chop finely.
2. Follow steps 1 and 2 from the Hot Water Bath Method (see page 28).
3. Add all ingredients to a stockpot and simmer, stirring frequently for 20 minutes.
4. Fill hot, sterilized pint jars (473 ml), leaving a ½-inch (1.3 cm) headspace.
    Clean rims and any spills with sterile cloth. Secure lids and rings.
5. Process pints (473 ml) in a hot water bath for 25 minutes,
    adjusting for altitude if necessary (see page 29).
6. Remove from canner and let cool for 24 hours. Check seal and
    store. Refrigerate any unsealed jars and use within 2 weeks.

Variation: You can also make this with green tomatoes. It'll taste a bit different,
but still yummy, and it's a great way to use up tomatoes before the frost hits.

Ajiaco (Chicken and Corn Stew), Colombia

Makes 4 quarts (3.8 l)
Method: Pressure Canning

2 ½ lbs (1.1 kg) red potatoes
3 500 mg Vitamin C tablets
2 qts (1.9 l) water
1 chicken, cleaned, skinned,
   and cut into 8 pieces
3 t (15 g) salt, divided
3 t (15 g) ground black pepper, divided

8 C (1.9 l) chicken stock
4 C (946 ml) water
1 large onion, finely chopped
3 t (2 g) dried oregano
5 ears of corn, shucked, kernels
   removed from cob

1. Peel and cube red potatoes into ½-inch (1.3 cm) pieces. Crush three
   Vitamin C tablets in 2 quarts (1.9 l) of water. Soak potato pieces in
   this mixture for 2 minutes, leaving until you're ready to use them.
2. Season chicken with a teaspoon (5 g) each of salt and pepper.
3. Add chicken stock and water to pot. Bring to a boil. Add chicken pieces, onion,
   and oregano. Simmer for 20 minutes. Using tongs, transfer chicken to a plate.
4. Drain potatoes. Add potatoes and corn to soup. Simmer for 5 minutes.
5. Remove bones from chicken and shred the meat.
6. Divide chicken evenly between the hot, sterilized quart jars (946 ml).
   Using a slotted spoon, divide potato and corn mixture between
   jars (chicken and vegetable mix should fill the jars halfway). Fill the
   jars with the remaining liquid, leaving a 1-inch (2.5 cm) headspace.
   You can heat some additional chicken stock or add boiling water
   to the jars if you need more liquid. Wipe rims and secure lids.
7. Follow canning steps 3–6 of the Pressure Canning Method on pages 60–61.
   Process quarts (946 ml) for 90 minutes in a pressure canner at pressure listed
   for your altitude and canner (see page 64).

Ballymore Stew, Ireland

Makes 4 quarts (3.8 l)
Method: Pressure Canner

This makes a great alternative to corned beef and hash for St. Patrick's Day.

1 lb (454 g) red boiling potatoes
3 500 mg Vitamin C tablets
2 qts (1.9 l) water
2 T (30 ml) olive oil
1 ½ lbs (680 g) lamb, cut
  into stewing chunks
2 onions, chopped
4 garlic cloves, minced
8 C (1.9 l) beef stock

1 can stout beer (e.g., Guinness)
2 C (473 ml) water
2 T (3 g) rosemary leaves
2 T (3 g) dried thyme
2 bay leaves
2 T (30 g) salt
2 t (10 g) ground pepper
8 carrots, sliced

1. Peel and cube potatoes into 1-inch (2.5 cm) pieces. Crush Vitamin C tablets in 2 quarts (1.9 l) of water and soak potatoes to prevent discoloration. Keep potato cubes in solution until you're ready to use them.
2. Heat oil in a stockpot over medium-high heat. Add the lamb pieces in two batches—cook until all sides are browned, about 2 minutes or so per side.
3. Place all lamb in the pot, adding onions and garlic. Sauté for 3 minutes. Add the stock, stout, water, and spices. Bring to a boil, then simmer for 20 minutes. Add potatoes and carrots. Simmer for an additional 2 minutes.
4. Using a slotted spoon, divide meat and vegetables evenly into hot canning jars, filling halfway. Top off the jars with the remaining soup liquid, leaving a 1-inch (2.5 cm) headspace. If you need more liquid, boil additional stock or water and add to the jars. Wipe rims and secure lids.
5. Follow canning steps 3–6 of the Pressure Canning Method on pages 60–61. Process quarts (946 ml) for 90 minutes in a pressure canner at pressure listed for your altitude and canner (see page 64).

Borscht, Ukraine

Makes 5 quarts (4.7 l)
Method: Pressure Canning

This soup is a staple of many eastern and central European culinary traditions. Variations exist, but here's the basic recipe popular in the Ukraine. It works well for canning.

3 500 mg Vitamin C tablets
2 qts (1.9 l) water
1 lb (453 g) potatoes, peeled and cubed
2 t (10 ml) olive oil
1 ½ lbs (680 g) stewing beef, cut
  into ¾-inch (2 cm) cubes
12 C (2.8 l) beef stock (this recipe
  is best with homemade stock)
12 beets (about 2 lbs [907 g]), peeled
  and cut into ½-inch (1.3 cm) strips

1 lb (453 g) tomatoes, peeled,
  seeded, and chopped
1 yellow onion, chopped
2 medium carrots, minced
1 green pepper, minced
⅛ C (30 ml) lemon juice
⅛ C (30 ml) red wine vinegar
1 t (5 g) black pepper
2 t (8 g) sugar

1. Dissolve Vitamin C pills in 2 quarts (1.9 l) of water and soak potatoes to prevent discoloration—this is an important step. Soak potatoes for at least 2 minutes, leaving them until you're ready to use them.
2. Heat olive oil in a stockpot over medium-high heat. Brown the beef on all sides, in batches if necessary. Add beef stock and vegetables and bring to a boil. Reduce heat and simmer for 15 minutes. Add lemon juice, vinegar, pepper, and sugar.
3. Pour into hot, sterilized canning jars. Leave a 1-inch (2.5 cm) headspace. Wipe rims and secure lids.
4. Follow canning steps 3–6 of the Pressure Canning Method on pages 60–61. Process pints (473 ml) for 40 minutes, quarts (946 ml) for 50 minutes in a pressure canner at pressure listed for your altitude and canner (see page 64).
5. Serve warm with sour cream, chopped parsley, chopped dill, and a hard-boiled egg.

Brazilian Black Bean Soup, Brazil

Makes 5 quarts (4.7 l)
Method: Pressure Canner

The orange flavor makes this medium-spicy bean soup stand out!

5 C (1 kg) dried black beans
3 medium onions, diced
10 garlic cloves, minced
2 T (15 g) ground cumin
2 T (15 g) salt
1 t (5 g) black pepper
1 t (2 g) cayenne pepper (or more to taste)
3 C (711 ml) orange juice

3 C (711 ml) vegetable stock
4 C (946 ml) water
4 medium carrots, diced
2 bell peppers, diced (green, red and
  yellow bell peppers all work great)
2 medium sweet potatoes, diced
5 medium tomatoes, skins
  removed, seeded, and diced

1. Cover black beans in water and soak overnight. Drain.
2. Add black beans to a stockpot with 8 cups (1.9 l) of fresh water. Bring to a boil, then reduce heat to simmer for 30 minutes. Drain.
3. In another pot, add onion, garlic, and ½ cup (118 ml) of water. Cook at medium heat for 3 minutes.
4. Add cumin, salt, and black and cayenne pepper, along with orange juice, vegetable stock, and water. Bring to a simmer and cook for 5 minutes. Add carrots, bell peppers, sweet potatoes, and tomatoes. Bring to a boil and cook for 5 minutes.
5. Divide cooked black beans evenly among hot, sterilized quart jars (946 ml). Ladle in soup mixture, leaving a 1-inch (2.5 cm) headspace. If additional liquid is needed, add boiling water. Wipe rims and secure lids.
6. Follow canning steps 3–6 of the Pressure Canning Method on pages 60–61. Process quarts (946 ml) for 90 minutes in a pressure canner at pressure listed for your altitude and canner (see page 64).

Lentil and Kielbasa Soup, Poland

Makes 5 quarts (4.7 l)
Method: Pressure Canner

A hearty meal in a bowl!

2 ½ C (302 g) dried lentils, rinsed
1 ½ lbs (680 g) kielbasa (smoked sausage), sliced into ½-inch (1.3 cm) pieces
2 large onions, chopped
5 carrots, chopped
7 garlic cloves, chopped
6 lbs (2.7 kg) tomatoes, peeled, seeded, and chopped
¼ C (7 g) dried parsley
1 ½ T (2 g) ground cumin
2 ½ T (18 g) paprika
1 T (15 g) salt
5 C (1 l) chicken or vegetable stock
2 t (10 g) ground pepper

1. Add lentils and 8 cups (1.9 l) of water to a stockpot. Bring to a boil and boil for 2 minutes. Set aside to soak for an hour.
2. Drain lentils. Add 8 cups (1.9 l) of fresh water, return to a boil, then strain, reserving lentil water. Transfer lentils to hot, sterilized quart jars (946 ml), filling each jar a quarter full.
3. Add remaining ingredients and lentil water to a stockpot and simmer for 15 minutes.
4. Divide vegetables and sausage into jars. Top off with soup liquid, leaving a 1-inch (2.5 cm) headspace. If necessary, add additional boiling water to jars to fill. Secure lids and rings.
5. Follow canning steps 3–6 of the Pressure Canning Method on pages 60–61. Process in a pressure canner for 90 minutes at pressure listed for your altitude and canner (see page 64).

Masoor Dal Soup, India

Makes 5 pints (2.4 l)
Method: Pressure Canner

2 ½ C (503 g) dried split red lentils
1 medium yellow onion, chopped
3 carrots, sliced
2 garlic cloves, minced
6 C (1.4 l) vegetable or chicken stock
1 lemon, sliced and seeded
1 T (2 g) curry powder (use a good quality)
1 t (5 g) freshly grated ginger
2 bay leaves

1. Hydrate lentils. Add lentils and 8 cups (2 l) of water to a stockpot.
    Bring to a boil and boil for 2 minutes. Set aside to soak for an hour.
2. Drain lentils. Add 8 cups (2 l) of fresh water, return to a boil,
    then strain, reserving lentil water. Transfer lentils to hot, quart-
    sized (946 ml) sterilized jars, filling each jar halfway.
3. Add onions, carrot, and garlic to stockpot with ½ cup
    (118 ml) of water. Cook for 3 minutes.
4. Add stock, 4 cups (946 ml) reserved lentil water, lemons, and spices to
    pot. Bring to a boil. Cover, reduce heat, and cook for 15 minutes. Add
    tomatoes and cook for 5 minutes. Remove lemon slices and bay leaves.
5. Ladle soup broth over lentils in canning jars, leaving a 1-inch
    (2.5 cm) headspace. Wipe rims and secure lids.
6. Follow canning steps 3–6 of the Pressure Canning Method on pages
    60–61. Process pints (473 ml) for 75 minutes and quarts (946 ml) for
    90 minutes at pressure listed for your altitude and canner (see page 64).
7. To serve, heat and garnish with fresh cilantro and a pinch of garam masala.

Minestrone, Italy

Makes 7 quarts (6.6 l)
Method: Pressure Canner

½ lb (227 g) dried white beans
   (great northern)
½ lb (227 g) potatoes (red, boiling type)
¼ C (57g) pancetta, chopped
1 t (5 ml) olive oil
1 onion, chopped
4 garlic cloves, minced
2 carrots, cut into ½-inch (1.3 cm) cubes
1 lb (454 g) yellow summer squash
½ lb (227 g) green beans cut into ½-inch (1.3 cm) lengths
2 lbs (907 g) tomatoes (skinned, seeded, and chopped)
8 C (2 l) chicken stock
2 t (1 g) dried oregano
1 T (2 g) dried basil
1 T (15 g) salt
2 t (10 g) pepper
Kale, chopped to garnish
Grated Parmesan cheese to garnish

1. Rehydrate beans by boiling them in 8 C (2 l) of water for 2 minutes. Remove from heat, let beans soak for an hour (or overnight). Drain, rinse beans, and cook in 8 cups (2 l) of fresh water on low heat for 30 minutes.
2. Meanwhile, peel potatoes and cut into ½-inch (1.3 cm) cubes. Place in a large bowl filled with 2 quarts (2 l) of water and three crushed 500 mg Vitamin C tablets. Keep in solution until ready to use (this step is important; skip it and the potatoes turn gray).

Soups and Stews

(Minestrone, continued from page 89.)

3. Heat a large stockpot over medium heat. Add olive oil and sauté pancetta for 4–5 minutes. Add onion and garlic. Cook for 3–5 minutes. Add remaining vegetables, stock, herbs, salt, and pepper. Cook for 10 minutes.
4. Add cooked beans to seven quart-sized (946 ml) jars, dividing equally. Using a slotted spoon, ladle vegetables from soup into hot, sterilized canning jars until jars are half full. Divide remaining soup stock between the jars. Top with boiling water, leaving a 1-inch (2.5 cm) headspace.
5. Follow canning steps 3–6 of the Pressure Canning Method (see pages 60–61). Process for 90 minutes in a pressure canner at pressure listed for your altitude and canner (see page 64).
6. To serve, warm soup with some added chopped kale. Top with grated Parmesan cheese.

Variation: You can easily make this meal vegetarian by omitting the pancetta and using vegetable stock.

Ropa Vieja, Cuba

Makes 4 quarts (3.8 l)
Method: Pressure Canner

A flavorful beef stew popular in Cuban cuisine.

2 lbs (907 g) skirt or flank steak, cut
   into 4-inch (10 cm) chunks
8 C (2 l) water
2 carrots, chopped
1 onion, chopped
2 ribs of celery, chopped
1 bay leaf
6 garlic cloves
2 t (1 g) dried oregano
2 t (1 g) ground cumin

2 t (10 g) salt
1 t (6 g) black peppercorns
2 green peppers, cut into strips
2 red bell peppers, cut into strips
2 yellow peppers, cut into strips
1 red onion, cut into ¼-inch
   (6.4 mm) strips
1 ½ lbs (680 g) tomatoes, skinned,
   seeded, and chopped

1. Combine beef, water, carrots, onion, celery, bay leaf, 3 garlic cloves (crushed), a teaspoon (542 mg) of oregano, a teaspoon (542 mg) of cumin, a teaspoon (5 g) of salt and peppercorns in a large stockpot and bring to a simmer. Simmer 30 minutes.
2. Transfer meat onto a large plate. Shred into bite-sized pieces.
3. Pour soup liquid through a strainer into a bowl. Discard solids. Return liquid to pot. Bring to a boil. Simmer 30 minutes until liquid is reduced by half. Add peppers, tomatoes, red onion, 3 garlic cloves (minced), a teaspoon (542 mg) of oregano, a teaspoon (542 mg) of cumin, a teaspoon (5 g) of salt, and a teaspoon (5 g) of ground pepper. Simmer 10 minutes.
4. Divide meat evenly among hot, sterilized jars, filling each jar a third full. Using a slotted spoon, divide vegetables among jars. Ladle liquid into jars, filling to leave a 1-inch (2.5 cm) headspace (use boiling water if you need extra liquid).
5. Follow canning steps 3–6 of the Pressure Canning Method on pages 60–61. Process quarts (946 ml) for 90 minutes in a pressure canner at pressure listed for your altitude and canner (see page 64).

Simple Boeuf Bourguignon, France

Makes 4 quarts (3.8 l)
Method: Pressure Canner

This simplified version of the famous French recipe (beef in red wine sauce) is easy to make and great to have on hand.

4 oz (113 g) bacon, diced
3 lbs (1.4 kg) stewing beef, cut into cubes
1 carrot, sliced
2 onions, sliced
5 large tomatoes, crushed, with skins and seeds removed
4 C (948 ml) red wine
4 C (948 ml) beef stock
4 C (948 ml) water
2 bay leaves
3 garlic cloves, minced
1 t (542 mg) thyme
3 t (15 g) salt
1 t (5 g) pepper

1. In a large stockpot, cook bacon at medium-high heat. Add beef cubes and brown on all sides (cook in batches to ensure proper browning).
2. Add carrot, onion, tomatoes, wine, stock, water, bay leaves, garlic, thyme, salt, and pepper. Bring to a boil. Reduce heat and cook at a low simmer for 50 minutes, stirring frequently. Remove bay leaves.
3. Using a slotted spoon, divide beef and vegetables evenly into quart (946 ml) or pint (473 ml) jars, filling jars two-thirds full. Top off jars with soup liquid, leaving a 1-inch (2.5 cm) headspace.
4. Follow canning steps 3–6 of the Pressure Canning Method on pages 60–61. Process quarts (946 ml) for 90 minutes and pints (473 ml) for 75 minutes at pressure listed for your altitude and canner (see page 64).

Stew with Chickpeas, Squash, and Sweet Potatoes, Morocco

Makes 4 quarts (3.8 l)
Method: Pressure Canner

2 ½ C (503 g) dried chickpeas
2 onions, diced
6 garlic cloves, minced
½ C (118 ml) water
1 ½ T (2 g) ground cumin
2 sticks cinnamon, broken into
   1-inch (2.5 cm) pieces
1 t (542 mg) ground turmeric
8 C (1.9 l) vegetable or chicken stock
1 ½ lbs (680 g) sweet potatoes,
   skinned and cut into sticks

1½ lbs (680 g) butternut squash,
   skinned and cut into
   ½-inch (1.3 cm) cubes
3 lbs (1.4 kg) tomatoes, chopped
   with skins and seeds removed
1 T (15 g) salt
1 t (5 g) ground pepper
Chopped cilantro, brined green
   olives, and yogurt to garnish

1. Soak chickpeas overnight. Drain. Cook chickpeas in 8 C (1.9 l) of fresh water for 30 minutes over low heat. Drain and reserve cooking liquid.
2. Add onion, garlic, and water to a stockpot. Cook at medium heat for 3 minutes.
3. Add cumin, cinnamon sticks, turmeric, 3 cups (711 ml) of reserved chickpea cooking liquid, and stock. Cook for 10 minutes. Add sweet potatoes, butternut squash, tomatoes, salt, and pepper. Bring to a boil and simmer for 3 minutes.
4. Divide chickpeas evenly among hot, quart-sized canning jars. Using a slotted spoon, add potato and squash mixture to jars, bringing combined solids mixture to the halfway full mark on the jars. Fill jars with soup liquid, leaving a 1-inch (2.5 cm) headspace. If additional liquid is needed, add boiling water. Wipe rims and secure lids.
5. Follow canning steps 3–6 of the Pressure Canning Method on pages 60–61. Process quarts (946 ml) for 90 minutes in a pressure canner at pressure listed for your altitude and canner (see page 64).
6. Heat to serve and garnish with chopped cilantro, brined green olives, and yogurt.

Tex-Mex Vegetarian Chili, Southwestern United States

Makes 5 pints (2.4 l)
Method: Pressure Canner or Hot Water Bath (variation at end of recipe)

1 C (201 g) dried kidney beans
2 ½ lbs (1 kg) tomatoes, halved
1 onion, quartered
3 garlic cloves
½ green pepper, chopped
¼ jalapeño pepper

1 ½ t (813 mg) ground cumin
2 t (5 g) paprika
½ t (271 mg) dried thyme
½ t (271 mg) dried sage
1 t (542 mg) dried oregano
1 t (5 ml) hot sauce

1. Boil beans in 4 cups (946 ml) of water for 2 minutes. Remove
    from heat and let set for an hour or overnight. Rinse beans and
    simmer in 4 cups (946 ml) of fresh water for 30 minutes.
2. Arrange tomatoes, onion, garlic, green pepper, and jalapeño in
    one layer on baking sheet. Broil 2 inches (5 cm) from heat, turning
    frequently with tongs until skins start to char, about 10–15 minutes.
    Cool and remove skins and seeds from tomatoes and peppers.
3. Add roasted vegetables, spices, and hot sauce to a stockpot. Cook at
    a simmer for 10 minutes.
4. Divide beans evenly among hot, sterilized canning jars. Ladle vegetable
    mixture into jars, leaving a ½-inch (1.3 cm) headspace. Top each pint with a
    tablespoon of lemon juice.
5. Follow canning steps 3–6 of the Pressure Canning Method on pages 60–61.
    Process pints (473 ml) for 75 minutes or quarts (946 ml) for 90 minutes in a
    pressure canner, at pressure listed for your altitude and canner (see page 64).
6. To serve, heat chili. Mix a teaspoon of corn meal with a tablespoon of water.
    Stir mixture into a pint of chili. Serve topped with shredded cheese.

Variation: To can this recipe using the Hot Water Bath method, omit
the beans and simply add canned or rehydrated beans when serving the
chili. Process pints (473 ml) for 50 minutes, adjusting for altitude.

Tortilla Soup, Mexico

Makes 7 quarts (3.3 l)
Method: Pressure Canner

Kernels cut from 4 ears of corn
1 small onion, sliced
4 garlic cloves, peeled
1 lb (454 g) tomatoes, halved
1 poblano or banana pepper
1 guajillo pepper (dried, reconstituted,
   seeds removed)—other medium
   hot peppers may be substituted

12 C (2.8 l) chicken stock
2 t (1 g) ground cumin
1 t (542 mg) ground coriander
1 t (542 mg) dried oregano
1 lb (454 g) chicken breast,
   cut into strips
Corn tortillas, cut into strips
Sour cream

1. Place half of the corn, onion, garlic, tomato, and poblano (or banana) pepper in a single layer on a cookie sheet or roasting pan. Broil 2 inches (5 cm) from heat, turning the peppers periodically with tongs until their skins are slightly charred, about 10–15 minutes.
2. Soak guajillo pepper in hot water for 20 minutes. Remove seeds, drain.
3. Add roasted vegetables to blender and puree until smooth.
4. In a large, heavy-bottomed stockpot, combine puree, 12 cups (2.8 l) of chicken stock, and 12 cups (2.8 l) of water with chicken breast. Add kernels from remaining two ears of corn and spices. On medium heat, simmer for 20 minutes.
5. Using a slotted spoon, remove chicken and corn pieces from soup. Fill hot, sterilized jars a third full with corn and chicken pieces. Fill jars with remaining soup liquid and top off with boiling water if necessary, leaving a 1-inch (2.5 cm) headspace.
6. Follow canning steps 3–6 of the Pressure Canning Method (see pages 60–61). Process quarts (946 ml) for 90 minutes, at pressure listed for your altitude and canner (see page 64).
7. To serve, fry tortilla strips in 1 ½ inches (3.8 cm) of oil until light brown, or bake until crispy. Heat soup. Ladle into bowls and add tortilla strips and a dollop of sour cream.

Tom Yum Gai, Thailand

Makes 4–5 quarts (3.8–4.7 l)
Method: Pressure Canner

Tom Yum is one of the most famous Thai dishes, served widely in Thailand, Burma, Singapore, and Indonesia. This recipe is characterized by hot and sour flavors, and the ingredients can easily be found at specialty and Asian markets.

10 C (2.4 l) chicken stock
6 C (1.5 l) water
1-inch (2.5 cm) piece of galangal or ginger, sliced thin
5 kaffir lime leaves (available at ethnic markets—in a pinch, substitute lime zest)
3 stalks of lemon grass, cut into 1-inch (2.5 cm) pieces
2 T (30 ml) hot chili paste
5 small Thai or Serrano chilis, left whole
6 T (90 ml) fish sauce
9 T (135 ml) fresh lime juice
6 shallots, thinly sliced
3 Roma tomatoes, skinned, seeded, and chopped
1 C (151 g) carrots, sliced
1 lb (454 g) chicken breast, cut into strips 1 inch
   (2.5 cm) wide and 2 inches (5 cm) long

1. Bring stock and water to a boil in a stockpot. Add all ingredients. Simmer for 20 minutes.
2. Divide evenly among hot, sterilized quart jars (946 ml), adding one whole chili per jar (make sure chili is intact—if it breaks open, the soup will become quite hot). Top with boiling water if necessary, leaving a 1-inch (2.5 cm) headspace.
3. Follow canning steps 3–6 of the Pressure Canning Method on pages 60–61. Process for 90 minutes, adjusting for altitude if necessary (see page 64).
4. To serve, heat and top with cilantro leaves. Canned straw mushrooms may also be added.

Chana Masala, India

Makes 4 pints (2.3 l)
Method: Pressure Canner

2 ½ C (503 g) dried chickpeas
1 t (5 ml) canola oil
1 T (2 g) cumin seeds
1 ½ lbs (680 g) tomatoes, crushed
  with skins and seeds removed
2 C (474 ml) water, reserved
  from cooking chickpeas
2 C (474 ml) vegetable broth
2-inch (5 cm) piece of fresh ginger,
  peeled and grated to a pulp

3 garlic cloves, finely minced
1 ½ t (813 mg) turmeric
2 t (1 g) garam masala (a spice mix
  available in most ethnic markets)
2 t (1 g) ground cumin
1 T (2 g) ground coriander
¼ t (136 mg) cayenne (or to taste)
3 t (15 g) salt
Yogurt and chopped cilantro to garnish

1. Soak chickpeas overnight. Drain.
2. Cook chickpeas over low heat for 30 minutes using 8 cups (1.9 l) of water.
   Drain chickpeas, reserving 2 cups (474 ml) of the cooking water.
3. Add oil to stockpot and cook on medium-high until hot. Add cumin and
   cook for 30 seconds. Add tomatoes, water from chickpeas, vegetable
   stock, ginger, garlic, remaining spices, and salt. Simmer 10 minutes.
4. Divide chickpeas among hot, pint-sized canning jars, filling just over
   halfway. Fill jars with hot liquid, leaving a 1-inch (2.5 cm) headspace. Add
   additional boiling water if necessary to fill. Wipe rims and secure lids.
5. Follow canning steps 3–6 of the Pressure Canning Method on pages 60–61.
   Process pints (473 ml) for 75 minutes, quarts (946 ml) for 90 minutes in a
   pressure canner at pressure listed for your altitude and canner (see page 64).
6. To serve, heat in a saucepan. Cook until sauce is desired consistency (some
   like it thicker than others). Serve with yogurt and chopped cilantro.

Murgh Tikka Masala, India

Makes 3–4 pints (1.4–1.9 l)
Method: Pressure Canner

This is an easy, flavorful version of tikka masala. The
meat is simmered in the curry broth until soft.

2 onions, roughly chopped
9 garlic cloves, crushed
2-inch (5 cm) piece of
   gingerroot, sliced thin
½ C (375 ml) water
2 T (3 g) ground coriander
4 t (2 g) ground cumin
2 t (1 g) turmeric
¼ t (130 mg) cayenne
1 lb (454 g) tomatoes, skinned,
   seeded, and chopped

3 lbs (1.4 kg) chicken breast, skin
   removed, cut in chunks
3 C (711 ml) water
3 C (711 ml) chicken stock
Salt and pepper to taste
Lemon juice, yogurt, and garam
   masala (a spice mix available in
   most ethnic markets) to garnish

1. Puree onion, garlic, and ginger in a food processor or
    blender along with a cup (237 ml) of water.
2. Heat pureed mixture in a stockpot on medium. Add coriander, cumin,
    turmeric, and cayenne. Add the tomatoes. Cook while stirring for 5 minutes.
3. Add chicken, 2 cups (474 ml) of water, salt, and pepper. Simmer 20 minutes.
4. Ladle into hot jars, ensuring chicken is fully immersed. Leave a
    1-inch (2.5 cm) of headspace. Wipe rims and secure lids.
5. Follow canning steps 3–6 of the Pressure Canning Method on pages 60–61.
    Process pints (473 ml) for 75 minutes, quarts (946 ml) for 90 minutes in a
    pressure canner at pressure listed for your altitude and canner (see page 64).
6. Heat to serve and stir in ¼ cup (59 ml) of yogurt per quart (946 ml)
    and a pinch of garam masala. You can also add a bit more of the
    curry and cayenne spices at this point if you like more heat.

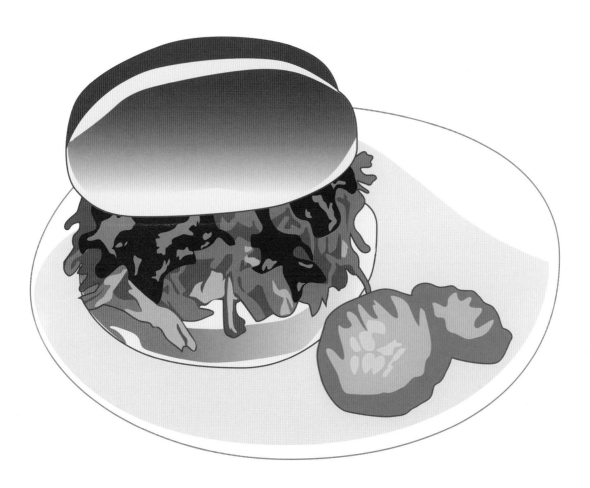

Pulled Pork with Carolina-Style BBQ Sauce, North Carolina

Makes 5–6 pints (2.4–2.8 l)
Method: Pressure Canner

Just pull this out of the pantry, heat, and serve as a
main dish or on buns for a great sandwich.

(Pulled Pork with Carolina-Style BBQ Sauce, continued from page 99.)

Tomato Barbecue Sauce

Makes 3 pints (1.4 l)

This is the sauce for the pork, but can
also be used for chicken and other meats.

1 lb (454 g) tomatoes, skins and
   seeds removed, crushed
2 ¼ C (532 ml) cider vinegar
1 C (237 ml) Worcestershire sauce
1 C (237 ml) apple juice
1 C (237 ml) pineapple juice
1 C (201 g) brown sugar

Pulled Pork
3–4 lb (1.4–1.8 kg) boneless
   pork shoulder roast
1 ¼ C (296 ml) cider vinegar, divided
1 onion, chopped
3 garlic cloves, minced
8 peppercorns

1. Stir together all BBQ sauce ingredients in a heavy-bottomed pan.
    Bring to a boil, reduce heat, and simmer for 5 minutes. Set aside.
2. Place pork in a large stockpot. Cover with water. Add ¾ cup (177 ml) of vinegar,
    onion, garlic, and peppercorns. Bring to a boil. Reduce heat and simmer,
    partially covered. Skim froth and add water as needed. Cook for 60 minutes.
3. Preheat oven to 350 degrees Fahrenheit. Transfer pork to a rack in a roasting
    pan. Pour ⅓ cup (79 ml) of vinegar over pork. Roast 45 minutes, turning every
    15 minutes. Transfer to a plate and let stand until cool enough to handle.
4. Reheat BBQ sauce.
5. Pull pork into shreds. Place into hot, sterilized pint (473 ml) jars. Ladle sauce over
    the top to fill the jar and fully cover the meat. Leave a 1-inch (2.5 cm) headspace.
6. Follow canning steps 3–6 of the Pressure Canning Method on
    pages 60–61. Process for 75 minutes in a pressure canner at
    pressure listed for your altitude and canner (see page 64).

Alsatian Spiced Red Cabbage, France

Makes 3–4 pints (1.9 l)
Method: Hot Water Bath

Variations of this recipe abound throughout the German-influenced sections of France, Bavaria, and eastern Europe. This blend of spices, sweet and tart, complete any fall or winter meal. Because the cabbage is only brined for 24 hours, it remains crisper, firmer, and less sour than sauerkraut.

(Alsatian Spiced Red Cabbage, continued from page 101.)

9 lbs (4 kg) red cabbage (about 3 heads)

3 tart apples

Spice mix: combine 2 T (about 11 g)
  each of whole cloves, whole allspice,
  peppercorns; and 3 sticks of cinnamon
  broken into small pieces. Tie mix
  into a piece of cheesecloth to
  create a bouquet garni

2 T (30 g) sea, pickling, or canning salt

3 500 mg Vitamin C tablets

2 qts (1.9 l) water

6 C (1.4 l) red wine vinegar

2 T (12 g) ground nutmeg

6 T (25 g) brown sugar

1 red onion, sliced

1. Slice cabbage into thin strips. Layer with salt in a large crock or
    glass bowl. Cover and let stand in a cool place for 24 hours.
2. The next day, follow canning preparation and processing
    instructions from the Hot Water Bath Method (see page 28).
3. Drain cabbage and rinse with cool water. Spin in a salad spinner
    or wrap in clean kitchen towels to remove excess liquid.
4. Core and chop apples into ½-inch (1.3 cm) pieces. Soak in an
    ascorbic acid mixture made by crushing three 500 mg Vitamin C
    tablets into 2 quarts (1.9 l) of water. Soak for at least 3 minutes
    and leave apples in solution until you're ready to use them.
5. In a large stockpot, combine apples with vinegar, spice bag, nutmeg, brown
    sugar, and onions. Bring to a boil then lower heat to simmer for 5 minutes.
6. Pack cabbage into hot, sterilized pint jars (473 ml), leaving
    1 ½ inches (3.8 cm) between the cabbage and the rim. Ladle hot
    liquid, apple, and onion mixture to cover cabbage, leaving a
    ½-inch (1.3 cm) headspace. Remove air bubbles and secure lid.
7. Process in a boiling hot water bath for 20 minutes,
    adjusting for altitude if necessary (see page 29).

Baked Beans, Boston, United States

Makes 7 quarts (6.6 l)
Method: Pressure Canner

This great version of a northeastern classic is adapted from a
recipe from the National Center for Home Preservation.

5 lbs (2.3 kg) kidney or navy beans
3 T (45 ml) molasses
1 T (15 ml) vinegar
2 t (10 g) salt
½ t (2.5 g) pepper

1 t (2 g) dry mustard
2 T (30 ml) Worcestershire sauce
¼ C (50 g) brown sugar
2 slices of bacon, divided into 7 1-inch
   (2.5 cm) pieces (approximately)

1. Add beans to a stockpot with water (3 cups [711 ml] of water
    for each cup [201 g] of dried beans). Bring to a boil and boil for
    2 minutes. Remove from heat and soak for an hour. Drain.
2. Add beans to a stockpot again with fresh water.
    Bring to a boil. Drain, reserving water.
3. To prepare molasses sauce, mix 5 cups (685 ml) of water from cooking
    liquid, molasses, vinegar, salt, pepper, mustard, Worcestershire
    sauce, and brown sugar in a saucepan. Heat to boiling.
4. Preheat oven to 350 degrees Fahrenheit. In a Dutch oven or
    other large casserole pan, add bacon and beans. Cover with
    molasses sauce. Bake for 4 hours, adding water as needed.
5. Fill hot, sterilized jars with bean mixture (can use quarts [946 ml] or pints
    [473 ml]), leaving a 1-inch (2.5 cm) headspace. Add additional boiling water if
    needed to ensure beans are submerged in liquid. Wipe rims and secure lids.
6. Follow canning steps 3–6 of the Pressure Canning Method on pages 60–61.
    Process quarts (946 ml) for 75 minutes and pints (473 ml) for 65 minutes in a
    pressure canner at pressure listed for your altitude and canner (see page 64).

Fasolakia (Green Beans in Tomato Sauce), Greece

Makes 4–5 pints (1.9–2.4 l)
Method: Pressure Canner

This recipe works great for canning, as authentic versions of the recipe call for a long cooking time and well-cooked beans.

2 T (30 ml) olive oil
2 onions, thinly sliced
8 lbs (3.6 kg) green beans, trimmed (traditionally, runner
  or pole beans are used in this recipe)
4 lbs (1.3 kg) tomatoes, skinned, seeded, and chopped
4 C (1 l) water
2 T (3 g) mint, chopped or 2 T (3 g) dried parsley
2 T (3 g) dried dill
Salt and pepper to taste

1. Heat olive oil over medium heat in a stockpot and sauté onion
    until soft. Add green beans and sauté 3–4 minutes.
2. Stir in tomatoes, water, herbs, salt, and pepper. Simmer 5 minutes.
3. Ladle into jars, leaving a 1-inch (2.5 cm) headspace. Top
    off with boiling water if necessary, to ensure beans are fully
    immersed in liquid. Wipe rims and secure lids.
4. Follow canning steps 3–6 of the Pressure Canning Method on pages 60–61.
    Process pints (473 ml) and quarts (946 ml) for 25 minutes
    in a pressure canner at pressure listed for your
    altitude and canner (see page 64).
5. Heat to serve and top with
    crumbled feta cheese.

Kimchi, Korea

Makes about 4 pints (1.9 l)
Method: Hot Water Bath

9 lbs (4.1 kg) Savoy cabbage
(3–4 large cabbages), washed and
cut into 2-inch (5 cm) pieces
10 T (150 g) coarse kosher salt
2 ½ C (593 ml) white rice vinegar
1 ½ C (356 ml) water
½ C (96 g) sugar

2 T (30 ml) chili pepper paste
(available at most Asian markets)
3 T (28 g) minced garlic
2 T (15 g) chili powder
2 T (29 g) minced fresh ginger
6 scallions, sliced in 1-inch
(2.5 cm) pieces

1. Layer cabbage with salt in a large bowl.
2. Transfer cabbage to a large, non-reactive colander (stainless-steel, ceramic, or plastic) placed over a large bowl. Cover with a plate weighted with a sealed quart jar (946 ml) filled with water. Keep at room temperature for 6–8 hours.
3. Follow canning preparation and processing instructions for the Hot Water Bath Method (see page 28).
4. Drain and rinse cabbage mixture. Soak in clean water for 15 minutes. Rinse again and remove excess water by spinning in a salad spinner or drying with kitchen towels.
5. In a saucepan, mix together the vinegar, water, sugar, chili paste, garlic, chili powder, and ginger in a large, non-reactive bowl. Bring to a boil, then lower heat to simmer for 10 minutes. Add scallions. Simmer for 2 additional minutes.
6. Add the cabbage to hot, sterilized pint jars (473 ml). Fill jars with hot liquid mixture, leaving a ½-inch (1.3 cm) headspace. Remove air bubbles, Secure lids.
7. Process in a hot water bath for 20 minutes, adjusting for altitude if necessary (see page 29).

Rodbetor, Sweden

Makes 5–6 pints (2.4–2.8 l)
Method: Hot Water Bath

Pickled beets with caraway, cloves, and red onion slices are a classic side dish in Scandinavia. Enjoy this sweet, sour, and flavor-packed treat.

3 lbs (1.4 kg) beets
2 t (10 g) salt
9 whole cloves
1 T (2 g) caraway seeds
2 C (474 ml) red wine vinegar
1 C (237 ml) white vinegar
1 C (237 ml) water
1 C (192 g) sugar
1 red onion, sliced into thin rings

1. Follow canning preparation and processing instructions for the Hot Water Bath Method (see page 28).
2. Scrub beets. Remove tops if they're still attached, leaving an inch (2.5 cm) of stem. Place beets in stockpot, cover with water, add salt, and bring to a boil. Reduce to a simmer and cook for 20–30 minutes until just tender. Run beets under cold water, slip off skins, and cut into ⅛-inch (3.2 mm) slices.
3. Tie cloves and caraway seeds in cheesecloth and place in stockpot. Add vinegars, water, sugar, and onion. Bring to a boil, then simmer for 15–20 minutes. Strain syrup to remove solids.
4. Pack beets into hot, sterilized jars and cover with syrup, leaving a ½-inch (1.3 cm) head-space. Wipe rims and secure lids.
5. Process pints (473 ml) for 30 minutes in a hot water bath, adjusting for altitude if necessary (see page 29).

Sauerkraut, Germany

Makes 4 pints (1.9 l)
Method: Hot Water Bath

Get ready for Octoberfest! Homemade sauerkraut is better than what you find in the stores and relatively easy to make. Crocks are made for this purpose—but you can use any 5-gallon or larger stone, glass, or food-grade plastic container. This recipe is very similar to the dill pickle recipe on pages 52–53.

10 lbs (4.5 kg) green cabbage (2–3 cabbages)
6 T (90 g) sea, pickling, or canning salt

To Ferment
1. Slice cabbage, in thin shreds, into your container. Add salt as you go—the salt will pull out the liquids and create the brine.
2. Mix thoroughly and let stand for 15 minutes.
3. Press down on the cabbage, bringing the juice to the surface. Repeat several times until brine fully covers the cabbage. If necessary, dissolve a tablespoon of salt into a cup of boiling water, cool to room temperature, and add to cabbage mixture.
4. Place a clean, inverted plate over the cabbage mixture, weighing it down with two quart-sized jars (946 ml) securely filled with water. (Cabbage needs to remain under the brine during the entire fermentation process.) Cover container with a clean cloth and set aside in a cool place. Check daily, removing any scum from the surface. Gas bubbles will form when fermentation starts. When bubbling ceases, this step of the process is done. Fermentation will take 4–6 weeks, depending on seasons, temperatures, and the produce. You can taste it to see if it's ready.

(Sauerkraut, continued from page 107.)

To Preserve
Once fermented, the cabbage may be eaten
immediately or canned for future meals.

5. Follow canning preparation and processing instructions
    from the Hot Water Bath Method (see page 28).
6. In a large stainless-steel or enamel stockpot, slowly bring
    sauerkraut and brine to a simmer, but do not boil.
7. Pack into hot, sterilized jars, leaving a ½-inch (1.3 cm)
    headspace. Make sure cabbage is covered by the brine.
8. Process pints (473 ml) for 10 minutes, quarts (946 ml) for
    15 minutes, adjusting for altitude if necessary (see page 29).

Sherry-Braised Turnips, England

Makes 5 quarts or 10 pints (4.7 l)
Method: Pressure Canner

This recipe, which appeared in *Saveur*, Issue #110, has been adapted here for canning.

2 qts (1.9 l) cold water
3 500 mg Vitamin C tablets, crushed
12 lbs (12.4 kg) turnips, peeled and
   cut into ½-inch (1.3 cm) cubes
4 apples, peeled and cut into
   ½-inch (1.3 cm) cubes
5 C (1.2 l) water

4 C (946 ml) sherry
1 T (6 g) ground nutmeg
1 T (8 g) dried ginger
1 T (8 g) ground cinnamon
1 t (5 g) ground pepper
1 T (13 g) brown sugar
Canning salt

1. Fill large bowl with 2 quarts (1.9 l) of cold water and stir in three crushed 500 mg Vitamin C tablets. Add cubed turnips and apples. Let sit for 3 minutes, leaving fruit and vegetables in solution until you're ready to use them.
2. In a stockpot combine sherry, sugar, nutmeg, ginger, cinnamon, pepper, and brown sugar. Bring to a boil.
3. Add turnips and apples. Simmer for 5 minutes.
4. Spoon turnips and apples into pint (473 ml) or quart (946 ml) jars. Pour liquid over the top, filling to leave a 1-inch (2.5 cm) headspace. If necessary, top with boiling water to fill jars. Add salt: ½ teaspoon (2.5 g) for pints, a teaspoon (5 g) for quarts.
5. Follow canning steps 3–6 of the Pressure Canning Method on pages 60–61. Process, using a pressure canner, 30 minutes for pints (473 ml) and 35 minutes for quarts (946 ml), at pressure listed for your altitude and canner (see page 64).
6. To serve, sauté parsnips and apples in a bit of butter until warm. Enjoy!

All-American Fruit Crisp

2 qts (1.9 l) Nectarine-Raspberry Preserves (see page 121 for recipe)
1 T (10 g) cornstarch
¾ C (190 g) all-purpose flour
¾ C (60 g) quick oats
¼ C (50 g) dark brown sugar
¼ t (628 mg) ground cinnamon
¼ t (628 mg) ground cardamom
5 T (72 g) butter, melted

1. Preheat oven to 375 degrees Fahrenheit and butter a 9" x 9" glass baking dish.
2. Strain fruit from jars and add to baking dish, stirring in cornstarch.
3. To make topping, combine flour, quick oats, dark brown sugar, cinnamon, and cardamom in a bowl. Add melted butter and mix until small clumps form.
4. Sprinkle topping over fruit and bake for 50 minutes.

Cognac Cherries, France

Makes 4 pints or 8 half-pints (1.9 l)
Method: Hot Water Bath

6 C (596 g) cherries
3 500 mg Vitamin C tablets
½ g (1.9 l) water
2 C (383 g) sugar
2 T (30 ml) lemon juice
1 ½ C (356 ml) white grape juice
3 C (711 ml) water
1 ½ C (356 ml) cognac
Zest of an orange

1. Pit cherries and soak in ascorbic acid mix (three Vitamin C tablets crushed into ½ gallon [1.9 l] of water).
2. Combine sugar, lemon juice, grape juice, and water in a saucepan and bring to a boil. Reduce heat and simmer for 5 minutes.
3. Add cherries and cook at a simmer for 5 minutes. Remove from heat. Add cognac.
4. Fill sterilized jars with cherries and orange zest. Pour hot syrup over cherries, leaving a ½-inch (1.3 cm) headspace. Remove air bubbles. Secure lids and rings.
5. Process in a hot water bath for 15 minutes, adjusting for altitude if necessary (see page 29).

Desserts

Fruit Soup, Sweden

Makes 4–5 pints (1.9–2.4 l)
Method: Hot Water Bath

Fruit soup is popular throughout Scandinavia. It's great anytime!

1 qt (946 ml) water
Rind from a lemon
1 C (210 g) long grain white rice*
4 cinnamon sticks
2 firm apples (Fuji, Granny Smith, Fireside, and other pie apples are a good choice)
1 lb (454 g) raspberries
3 500 mg Vitamin C tablets
2 qts (1.9 l) water
1 qt (946 ml) apple juice
2 lbs (907 g) cherries, pitted
3 T (36 g) sugar or 5 T (75 ml) honey

1. Follow canning preparation and processing instructions
    from the Hot Water Bath Method (see page 28).
2. Add water, rice, lemon rind, and cinnamon sticks to a stockpot.
    Simmer for 20 minutes. Strain, saving the infused water.
3. Press raspberries through a fine sieve to remove seeds.
4. Peel, core, and dice apples. Crush three 500 mg
    Vitamin C tablets into 2 quarts [1.9 l] of water.
5. Soak apples in this ascorbic acid solution for 2 minutes,
    leaving until you're ready to use them.
6. Return the infused water to the stove, add apple juice, and bring to a simmer.

* The rice in this recipe is used to infuse the water with flavor. Since the rice
  itself does not go into the jars, it is safe to can this recipe.

7. Add apples, cherries, and sugar or honey. Simmer for 5 minutes. Add raspberry pulp. Simmer an additional 2–3 minutes.
8. Ladle into hot, sterilized pint jars, leaving a ½-inch (1.3 cm) headspace. Wipe rims and secure lids.
9. Process in a hot water bath for 10 minutes, adjusting for altitude if necessary (see page 29).
10. To serve, chill jars for use in refrigerator for 6 or more hours. Pour into bowls and top with fresh whipped cream (sweetened to taste) or, more traditionally, sour cream. Yum!

Variations: You can substitute other berries, such as blueberries, blackberries, and so on, for the cherries and raspberries.

Higos al Brandy, Spain

Makes 7 pints (3.3 l)
Method: Hot Water Bath

6 C (1.4 l) water
3 C (711 ml) white grape juice
1 C (192 g) sugar
Zest from 2 oranges
2 sprigs fresh rosemary (or 2 T [3 g] dried)
8 lbs (3.6 kg) figs, washed and drained

1 C (237 ml) brandy
½ C (118 ml) dry sherry
3 ½ T (53 ml) lemon juice
Almond slivers and whipped
   cream to garnish

1. Follow canning preparation and processing instructions
   for the Hot Water Bath Method (see page 28).
2. Combine water, grape juice, sugar, orange zest, and rosemary in a
   stockpot. Bring to a boil, then lower heat to simmer. Simmer uncovered
   for 15 minutes until liquid becomes thicker and a bit syrupy.
3. Add figs and simmer for 4 more minutes. Stir in brandy
   and sherry. Cook for an additional minute.
4. Use a slotted spoon to remove figs from pan and add to sterilized pint (237 ml)
   jars. Strain solids from syrup. Ladle syrup into jars, leaving a ½-inch (1.3 cm)
   headspace. Add 1 ½ t (8 ml) lemon juice to each jar.
5. Secure lids and rings. Process in a hot water bath for 45 minutes,
   adjusting for altitude if necessary (see page 29).
6. Serve figs on a plate with syrup, warm or cooled in the refrigerator.
   Garnish with toasted almond slivers and/or whipped cream.

Italian Plums, Italy

Makes 4–5 pints (1.9–2.4 l)
Method: Hot Water Bath

6 lbs (3 kg) plums
1 t (2 g) whole cloves
1 small knob of ginger, peeled, and cut into ⅛-inch (3 mm) slices
2 ½ C (479 g) sugar
1 C (201 g) light brown sugar
½ C (118 ml) orange juice
3 C (711 ml) white balsamic vinegar
2 C (474 ml) water

1. Follow canning preparation and processing instructions
   from the Hot Water Bath Method (see page 28).
2. Wash and prick plums, setting aside in a glass or food-grade plastic bowl.
3. In a large saucepan, blend all other ingredients and bring to a boil. Simmer
   syrup 10 minutes. Cool 20–30 minutes. Using a strainer, pour syrup over
   plums. Cover bowl and set overnight (at least 8 hours) at room temperature.
4. Separate syrup from plums and add to a stockpot, then
   bring to a boil. Add plums, simmer for 15 minutes.
5. Add plums, and enough syrup to cover them, to hot, sterilized, pint jars
   (237 ml), leaving a ½-inch (2.5 cm) headspace. Process in a hot water
   bath for 15 minutes, adjusting for altitude if necessary (see page 29).
6. Let cure for three weeks prior to serving.

Port Poached Pears, Portugal

Makes 4 quarts or 7 pints (3.3 l)
Method: Hot Water Bath

3 C (711 ml) port
2 C (474 ml) pinot noir (or another dry
   red wine)
3 C (711 ml) grape juice
3 C (711 ml) water
1 C (192 g) sugar
2 cinnamon sticks

2 star anise
10 peppercorns
Zest from a lemon
10 lbs (4.5 kg) firm (yet ripe) pears,
   peeled, cored, and halved
6 500 mg Vitamin C tablets
1 g (4.8 l) cold water

1. Follow canning preparation and processing instructions
   for the Hot Water Bath Method (see page 28).
2. Combine port, pinot noir, grape juice, water, and sugar in a stockpot. Bring
   to a boil. Reduce heat and add cinnamon sticks, star anise, peppercorns,
   and lemon zest. Simmer for 15 minutes until the mixture becomes syrupy.
3. In the meantime, dissolve the Vitamin C tablets in a gallon (3.8 l)
   of cold water. Soak pear halves in this mixture for 5 minutes,
   leaving pears in solution until you're ready to use them.
4. Add pears to hot syrup and cook for 5 minutes at a simmer.
5. Remove pears and place in hot, sterilized jars. Strain syrup to remove
   solids. Ladle syrup into jars, leaving a ½-inch (1.3 cm) headspace.
6. Secure lids and rims. Process 20 minutes for pints (473 ml), 25 minutes
   for quarts (946 ml), adjusting for altitude if necessary (see page 29).

Serving Tip: Make a poached pear and baby greens salad. Simply remove pears
from the jar, arrange over greens, and add blue cheese and red onions. Make a
dressing by reducing the syrup and mixing with a bit of extra virgin olive oil.

Carrot and Daikon Pickle, Vietnam

Makes 6 half-pints (1.4 l)
Method: Hot Water Bath

Bring a bit of Asian flair to your table with these simple pickles.
Daikons (large, white Asian radishes) can be found at many farmers'
markets and are becoming more popular in produce sections.

1 lb (453 g) carrots, peeled and cut into matchsticks
3 lbs (1.4 kg) daikon radish, peeled and cut into matchsticks
4 t (20 g) kosher salt
1 C (192 g) sugar, divided
2 C (474 ml) rice vinegar
1 C (237 ml) warm water

1. Follow canning preparation and processing instructions
   for the Hot Water Bath Method (see page 28).
2. In a bowl, combine the carrots, daikon, salt, and a teaspoon (4 g) sugar.
   Let sit until the vegetables have wilted slightly and liquid pools at the
   bottom of the bowl, about 30 minutes. Drain vegetables; rinse and
   pat dry with paper towels. Transfer vegetables to a medium bowl.
3. In a saucepan, whisk together the remaining sugar, vinegar,
   and water. Bring to a boil, then simmer for 10 minutes.
4. Pack daikon radishes and carrots into hot, sterilized jars and cover with
   hot syrup, leaving a ½-inch (1.3 cm) headspace. Secure lids with rims.
5. Process half-pints (237 g) or pints (473 g) for 15 minutes in a hot
   water bath, adjusting for altitude if necessary (see page 29).

Lemon Grass Syrup, Thailand

Makes 4 pints (1.9 l)
Method: Hot Water Bath

There are hundreds of ways to use this versatile syrup. Try ladling it over cakes or fruit salads, or adding a tablespoon per glass to iced tea or lemonade.

3 C (575 g) sugar
3 C (711 ml) water
3 C (711 ml) white grape juice
8 lemon grass stalks (core only), sliced
4 lemon grass stalks (core only), cut to 3-inch (7.5 cm) pieces

1. Follow canning preparation and processing instructions
   for the Hot Water Bath Method (see page 28).
2. In a saucepan, combine sugar, water, grape juice, and lemon grass slices and
   pieces. Simmer over medium heat for 10 minutes, stirring frequently.
3. Using tongs, remove lemon grass stalk pieces from syrup
   and place into hot, sterilized canning jars.
4. Strain syrup to remove lemon grass slices. Pour into
   jars, leaving a ½-inch (1.3 cm) headspace.
5. Secure lids and rings. Process for 20 minutes in a hot water
   bath, adjusting for altitude if necessary (see page 29).

Fun cocktail ideas using lemongrass syrup:

Lemon Grass Mojito
In a cocktail shaker, combine 4 sprigs of fresh mint with a tablespoon (30 ml) of lemon grass syrup. Muddle mint and syrup (you can use the back of a spoon). Add a jigger (44 ml) rum and ½ cup (4 cubes) of ice. Shake and pour all into a tall glass. Top with club soda. Garnish with a small stalk of lemon grass.

Lemon Grass Gin Fizz

In a cocktail shaker, mix a tablespoon (15 ml) of lemon grass syrup, ¼ teaspoon (1 ml) of lime juice, and a jigger (44 ml) of gin. Shake and pour into a cocktail glass. Top with either tonic water or ginger ale. Garnish with a lime wedge.

Simple Rum Sipper

In a highball, mix a tablespoon (15 ml) of lemon grass syrup with a jigger (44 ml) of rum and juice from a fresh lime. Add ice and top with club soda for a refreshing cocktail.

119

Mango Chutney, Pakistan

Makes 8 half-pints (1.9 l)
Method: Hot Water Bath

A great side with many meals. We've toned down the spices in this
recipe—if you like it fiery hot, simply add more cayenne!

9 lbs (4 kg) green mangoes,
  peeled, pitted, and sliced
1 C (288 g) sugar
1 C (237 ml) grape juice
2 C (474 ml) cider vinegar
2 medium onions, chopped
2 red bell peppers, chopped
1 C (151 g) raisins

1 T (15 g) salt
1 ½ t (7 g) fresh ginger, finely chopped
¼ t (136 mg) cayenne
1 t (2 g) dry mustard
1 t (3 g) ground cinnamon
1 T (6 g) ground cloves
2 garlic cloves, minced
Juice from 2 limes, plus zest

1. Place mango slices flat on a baking sheet. Sprinkle with 2 teaspoons
   (10 g) of salt. Set aside for 8–12 hours (this removes the excess liquid).
2. Follow canning preparation and processing instructions
   for the Hot Water Bath Method (see page 28).
3. Add sugar, grape juice, and vinegar to a saucepan or stockpot.
   Bring to a boil, then reduce to simmer.
4. Dice mango.
5. Add mango and remaining ingredients to saucepan or stockpot.
   Simmer for 30–45 minutes, stirring often.
6. Ladle into hot, sterilized half-pint jars (237 ml), leaving a ¼-inch (6.4mm)
   headspace. Secure lids and rims.
7. Process in a hot water bath for 15 minutes, adjusting
   for altitude if necessary (see page 29).

Nectarine-Raspberry Preserves, United States

Makes 4 quarts (3.8 l)
Method: Hot Water Bath

These preserves can be eaten alone or used to make an
All-American Fruit Crisp. See page 110.

10 lbs (4.5 kg) nectarines, peeled and cut into bite-sized pieces
1 qt (946 ml) plus 6 C (1.4 l) water, divided
3 500 mg Vitamin C tablets
4 C (946 ml) apple or white grape juice
2 C water
½ C (118 ml) sugar
3 lbs (1.4 kg) raspberries, washed

1. Follow canning preparation and processing instructions
    for the Hot Water Bath Method (see page 28).
2. Soak nectarines in a solution of 1 quart (946 ml) water mixed
    with 3 crushed Vitamin C tablets for 2–3 minutes to prevent
    discoloration. Leave fruit in solution until ready to use.
3. Heat 6 cups (1.4 l) of water, grape juice, and sugar to a
    simmer. Add nectarines and cook for 5 minutes.
4. Use a slotted spoon to move nectarines from pan. Place in hot, sterilized
    quart (946 ml) jars. Add raspberries to jars. Fill with hot syrup. Add
    more boiling water if necessary, leaving a ½-inch (1.3 cm) headspace.
5. Secure lids and rings. Process in a hot water bath, 30 minutes for pints (473 ml),
    35 minutes for quarts (946 ml), adjusting for altitude if necessary (see page 29).

Tomato Taco Sauce, Mexico

Makes 7 pints (3.3 l)
Method: Hot Water Bath

20 lbs (9 kg) peeled, cored, finely
   chopped Roma tomatoes
2 garlic cloves, crushed
2 ½ C (379 g) chopped onions
2 jalapeño peppers, seeded and chopped
2 long green chilis, seeded and chopped
1 ½ C (356 ml) vinegar

1 T (15 g) salt
1 ½ T (23 g) black pepper
1 T (12 g) sugar
2 T (3 g) dried oregano
2 T (3 g) chopped cilantro
1 t (542 mg) ground cumin

Note: Do not add more onion or peppers than listed in this recipe unless you are using the pressure canner. These are low-acid vegetables and will reduce the acidity of the overall recipe to a level unsafe for hot water bath canning. The added vinegar is also important to this and all salsa/hot sauce recipes for home canning. Vinegar increases the overall acidity of salsa and hot sauce recipes to ensure safe canning.

1. Follow steps 1 and 2 from the Hot Water Bath Method (see page 28).
2. Add all ingredients to a stockpot and cook at a simmer, stirring frequently until mixture thickens, about an hour.
3. Puree in blender (be careful to only fill blender half full and use a towel to hold the lid down; hot liquids in blenders can be dangerous).
4. Fill sterilized pint jars (473 ml), leaving a ½-inch (1.3 cm) headspace. Clean rims and any spills with sterile cloth. Secure lids and rings.
5. Process pints (473 ml) in a hot water bath for 20 minutes, adjusting for altitude if necessary (see page 29).

Now that you can, invite your friends and family to join you. Canning parties are a fun way to make great food and lasting memories.

Ingredients:
 Friends and family
 Music, food, and beverages
 Your favorite items to can
 Jars, a stove, and a canning pot, and
 The Fresh Girls' Guide to Easy Canning DVD and book!

Enjoy the harvest season throughout the year.

 All the best,

 Ana Micka

Peach Jam

Spiced berry Jam

Roasted Spaghetti Sauce

Resources

Here are a few of my favorite sources for the latest, greatest information on canning and preserving methods.

Websites

National Center for Home Food Preservation
www.uga.edu/nchfp
Check out this site for the most current research-based canning information and guidelines.

From Farm to Table: University of Minnesota's Extension Service Food Preservation Resource Center
www.extension.umn.edu/foodsafety/components/foodpreservation.htm
University extension services are great resources for home canners. The University of Minnesota's Extension Service provides many links to other useful food preservation sites. To find the extension service near you, visit www.csrees.usda.gov/Extension

AnswerLine
www.extension.iastate.edu/answerline
This website, run by the University of Minnesota Extension and Iowa State University Extension, provides answers to questions on canning and other preservation methods.

Testing Pressure Canner Gauges
www.extension.umn.edu/foodsafety/components/pdfs/testingPressureCannerGauges.pdf
This link downloads a PDF that provides information on where to send your gauge to be tested.

Books

The Ball Blue Book of Preserving and the *Ball Complete Book of Home Preserving* by Judy Kingry and Lauren Devine provide an extensive collection of canning and preservation recipes and tips.

The Big Book of Preserving the Harvest by Carol Costenbader is a nicely designed and easy to access resource guide.

The Farmer's Wife Canning and Preserving Cookbook by Lela Nargi provides updated and tested recipes for old farm favorites.

Stocking Up: The Third Edition of America's Classic Preserving Guide by Carol Hupping. This book, published with the staff of the Rodale Food Center, includes many great suggestions for low-sugar and sugar-free recipes.

125

ch Jam

Nectarine-Raspberry
Preserves

Grape Jelly

Roasted
Spaghetti Sauce

Salsa

Potatoes

Spiced
Blueberry Jam

n Broth

Alsatian Spiced
Red Cabbage

Applesauce

Creamy
Squash Soup

About the Author

Ana Micka taught herself to can several years ago. It only made sense—in the cold climate of Minnesota, canning is the only way to eat fresh, locally grown food outside of our short harvest season. Soon, friends were asking her for advice. So, to save time and make it easy, she created an instructional DVD and guidebook showing and describing each step of the process. Ana's guidebook has been featured in the *Minneapolis Star Tribune*. She gives canning demonstrations for the Minnesota Horticultural Society and at local farmers' markets. In this expanded version of her original guidebook, Ana shares many more tips and recipes. Ana lives with her husband and daughter in St. Louis Park, Minnesota.